The Character Education **Handbook**

Lee Johnson

Establishing A Character Program in Your School

Anne C. Dotson & Karen D. Wisont

The Character Education Handbook
Establishing a Character Program in Your School
by Anne C. Dotson & Karen D. Wisont

Published by Character Press
P.O. Box 110356
Cleveland, Ohio 44111 U.S.A.
http://www.teachingcharacter.com
1.888.280.4390

All rights reserved. No part of this book may be reproduced or transmitted in any form or by any means, electronic or mechanical, including photocopying, recording, or by any information storage and retrieval system, without written permission from the publisher, except for the inclusion of brief quotations in a review.

Notice of liability:
The information in this book is distributed on an "as is" basis, without warranty. While every precaution has been taken in the preparation of this book, neither the authors nor Character Press shall have any liability to any person or entity with respect to any liability, loss, or damage caused or alleged to be caused directly or indirectly by the instructions contained in this book.

Copyright © 2001 by Anne C. Dotson and Karen D. Wisont

Cover design and book layout by Gregory Wisont

Publisher's Cataloging-in-Publication Data

Dotson, Anne C.
  The character education handbook : establishing a character program in your school / Anne C. Dotson and Karen D. Wisont. -- 1st ed.
     p. cm.
  Includes bibliographical references
  LCCN: 00-192087
  ISBN: 0-9704838-4-8
  1. Moral education. 2. Character--Study and teaching
--United States.   I. Wisont, Karen D.   II. Title.

LC311.D68 2001   370.11'4'0973
                                 QBI00-858

Acknowledgments

This book would not have come about without the support of Ray Dotson and Gregory Wisont. Ray provided steady encouragement and endless patience. Gregory made it happen, handling all the details that move a book from text document to printed product.

We gratefully acknowledge the efforts of Kevin Ryan, Tom Lickona, Melanie Mitchell, Hal Urban, and Janice Burroughs in reviewing this work. Roger Roudebush provided editorial advice. Elisa Martinez prepared illustrations that add a liveliness to the text. We also acknowledge the many experts in the fields of character education and team development who have contributed in a myriad of ways to our knowledge.

Foreword

Dr. Kevin Ryan
Author, *Building Character in Schools*
Center for the Advancement of Ethics and Character
Boston University School of Education
Boston, Massachusetts

As we move into this new century, the United States of America finds itself the most powerful country in the history of the world. We have riches, natural resources, and a large and talented population. We have vast military power and few strong enemies. We have a strong and vibrant economy and a huge jump on the rest of the world in technology. On the other hand, as Americans we have much unfinished business to do if we are to become the "City on the Hill" that our founders hoped we would become.

One of the greatest threats to our current good fortune and our future prosperity is the widespread failure of the adult community—parents, clergy, and teachers—to pass on to young people the core moral values which are the foundation of a good life and a good society. Many of our children have a weak understanding and grasp of virtues such as responsibility, respect, self-control, and honesty. For example, a recent study of 8,600 high students by the Josephson Institute, entitled "Report Card on the Ethics of American Youth," found the following:

- Cheating is extremely widespread. Seventy-one percent of all high school students admitted that they cheated on an exam at least once in the past 12 months; 45% said they did so two or more times.

- Lying is rampant. Ninety-two percent of students have lied to their parents in the past 12 months; 79% said they did so two or more times.

- Children are drunk in school. Nearly one in six students (16%) admitted that they have been drunk in school during the past year; 9% said they were drunk two or more times.

The author of the report claimed that there exists among students a "shocking level of moral illiteracy" and described the study results as further evidence of the thinning of our "moral ozone." These and other data paint a picture of young Americans who are disengaged from our moral heritage—those moral principles and good habits that in the past have characterized our nation.

Americans, however, are a very resilient and imaginative people. We have been characterized as having a "can do" spirit once we focus on an issue or problem. There are many signs that we, as a nation, are turning our attention back to the moral training of children. For some time now, national opinion polls have demonstrated that many parents are deeply concerned about an inability to pass on cherished values to their children. Our political leaders have picked up this concern. The 1980s cry of William Bennett for a renewed focus on character formation was picked up in the 1990s by President Clinton, who hosted an unprecedented five White House Conferences on the subject of Character Education. In the 2000 presidential contest, both candidates made character education a major tenant of their educational platforms. At the same time that political leaders were urging parents and teachers back to character education, the newly crowned Miss America took up character education as the flag under which she would fly during her twelve-month reign! Clearly we are at the Character Moment.

There is one weak link in the chain, however: America's teachers have been left out. Most teachers enter the profession wanting to help children acquire moral maturity, yet they find that their efforts to teach knowledge and skills are stymied by students' poor self-control and lack of responsibility. Character education has rarely been part of their teacher preparation. Studies done in the 1990s by the Boston University Center for the Advancement of Ethics and Character show that teacher educators are confused about what to do; deans and directors of teacher education overwhelming acknowledge doing little to prepare future teachers for the character formation aspects of their work. Similarly, teachers acknowledge receiving little or no training in moral or character education.

The Character Education Handbook enters and fills this information and training gap. Teachers and administrators will find very practical answers on how to translate their desire to be educators of character into everyday school and classroom realities. In a very concrete way, this book fills in the missing pieces of "how" to build and maintain a real-world program that bridges the gap between theory and practice, between good intentions and actual activities that will help children improve their lives by gaining the moral virtues that constitute good character.

Foreword

Dr. Tom Lickona
Author, *Educating for Character*
Director, Center for the 4th and 5th Rs (Respect and Responsibility)
Cortland, New York

"If we do not turn our children's hearts toward knowledge and character, we will lose their gifts and undermine their idealism."
—George W. Bush, inaugural address

"The beginning is the most important part."
— Plato

Wise societies since the time of Plato have made moral maturity a deliberate aim of schooling. They have educated for character as well as competence, decency as well as literacy, virtue as well as knowledge.

In this timely, practical, and well-written handbook, authors Anne Dotson and Karen Wisont document the resurgence of character education in our nation's schools. As we enter a new millennium, we're recovering ancient wisdom: without basic human virtues such as respect, responsibility, honesty, hard work, compassion, and self-control, we can't lead fulfilling lives, create safe and effective schools, or function harmoniously as communities.

Agreeing about the need for character education, however, turns out to be the easy part. The hard part is figuring out how to do it, and do it well.

In the past decade, there's been an explosion of good books and materials on the theory and practice of character education. The substance of educating for character—what it looks like in classrooms and schools—has been well-described. But what's been missing in the field is a user's manual—a step-by-step guide to the process of starting and sustaining a quality character education program. *The Character Education Handbook* fills that need.

Authors Dotson and Wisont point out that whatever the design of our character education program, a successful implementation process should involve six key groups: teachers, other school staff, parents, students, businesses, and community organizations.

For the past six years, our Center has sponsored a Summer Institute in Character Education for teams representing these constituencies. They say they go away with a truckload of good ideas but struggle with designing a plan of action. What are the first steps? How to share all this with others back home? How to get the rest of the school staff on board? What about students and parents?

In dealing with all these concerns, *The Character Education Handbook* will be an invaluable guide. Hats off to the authors for providing character educators everywhere with essential help for their enterprise.

Contents

Introduction 11

Chapter 1 Character Education: Making a Difference 17

Chapter 2 Getting Started in Character Education 23

Chapter 3 The First Meetings 41

Chapter 4 Choosing Your Teaching Approach 55

Chapter 5 Developing Student Advocates 67

Chapter 6 Cultivating Parent Support 79

Chapter 7 Involving the Community 85

Chapter 8 Building Excitement at Your School 93

Chapter 9 Finding Financial and Other Support 103

Chapter 10 Measuring the Effect of Character Education 109

Chapter 11 Improving the Program 119

Chapter 12 Optimizing Committee Dynamics 129

Post Script 149

Resource Guide 151

Contents

Introduction

If you are planning for a year, sow rice;
If you are planning for a decade, plant trees;
If you are planning for a lifetime, educate people.
—*Chinese proverb*

If you're a teacher, chances are good that you have heard of character education. The idea of teaching students basic character traits—such as responsibility, honesty, loyalty, and respect—has returned to the classroom in a big way. As of late 2000, the United States Department of Education had funded character programs in 28 states with grants of $1 million each, disbursed over four years. This funding is being used by the states, in conjunction with individual school districts, to integrate character education into their curricula by developing materials, providing teacher training, and involving parents in character education. An additional $2 million was made available in 2000.

To meet the grant requirements, many educators are finding themselves in the position of having to get a program going in short order. This can be an overwhelming task. *The Character Education Handbook* is designed to help sort out some of the details involved in establishing a character program and to suggest ideas for getting started.

When we first became involved in character education, the questions we heard focused on "what" and "why"—what is character education and why would anyone teach it in school? More recently, though, the questions have shifted toward "how":

The aim of this book is to provide a foundation for answering those "how" questions.

This book grew out of phone conversations between the authors: one working in business and the other teaching in an urban school.

- How do you implement the program?
- How do you run a committee?
- How do you get staff to support the program?
- How do you involve students, parents, and the community?
- How do you assess whether the program is effective?

The aim of this book is to provide a foundation for answering those "how" questions.

Much of the committee-oriented information in this book grew out of numerous conversations between the authors. As Anne was leading the efforts to implement character education in an urban school, Karen was working as a business consultant, facilitating workplace teams and leading workshops on how to be more effective in team collaborations. The application of business principles to school committees seemed natural to us. By using simple techniques that are common in business meetings, Anne observed that the character committee meetings became more effective, and as a result, the committee became more productive.

It can be overwhelming to be in charge of implementing a character program from scratch, yet each year more and more teachers find themselves in that situation. We hope this book will answer some of the questions you might encounter in the first few years of a character program. We don't claim to address every question you might have, nor do we think that there is only one way to implement a character program. There are as many ways to be successful with character education as there are schools.

How to Use This Book

If you wish, you can read the entire book from front to back; if you are leading a newly-formed character committee, this is the approach we recommend. Alternately, if your program is already functioning and you are looking for new ideas to enhance its effectiveness, you can start with the chapters that are most pertinent to your issues. Please take the ideas here and adapt them to your particular environment—use them as a starting place for your own creativity.

Chapter 1 presents a brief overview of the character education movement in the United States. Chapters 2 and 3 will help you get the basics in place: setting up a committee, figuring out your role as chairperson, and holding your first meetings. Chapter 4 discusses different options for incorporating a character message into your curriculum. Student involvement is the focus of chapter 5, and parent support is the theme of chapter 6. Chapter 7 provides ideas for involving community organizations and businesses in the character program. Chapter 8 addresses the topic of building excitement in your school. In chapter 9, we discuss the need for funding and how to go about finding financial and other support for the program. Chapter 10 covers the important issue of assessment. In chapter 11, you'll find ideas for improving the program from year to year. Because collaboration is vital to the success of the program, we've included suggestions for optimizing committee interactions in chapter 12. Finally, the resource guide will point you toward some of the many products and services available for use in character education.

You will notice that we use a hexagon symbol as an "anchor" for each page. This symbol represents the six key groups comprising a successful character education program:

1. **Parents,** who provide primary instruction in character education and are their children's greatest models;

2. **Teachers,** who provide reinforcement of character instruction and modeling;

3. **Students,** who provide peer leadership, influencing their friends and classmates;

4. **Staff,** who reinforce the character traits throughout the school day with students, other staff members, and outside visitors;

5. **Businesses,** who provide tangible and intangible support for the program;

6. **Community organizations,** who support and encourage the efforts of schools and families in developing good character among citizens.

Ultimately, the success of character education at any school depends on the synergistic efforts of these groups.

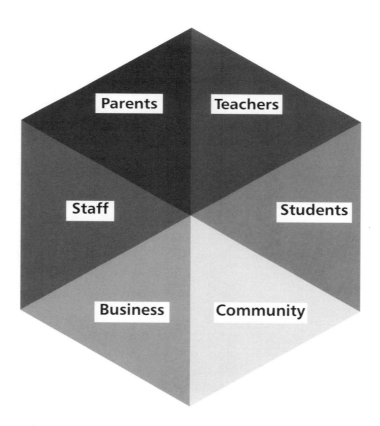

Each of these groups is an integral part of a successful character education program.

Chapter 1

Character Education: Making a Difference

"The only limit to our realization of tomorrow will be our doubts of today."
—*Franklin Delano Roosevelt*

Character education is an idea whose time has come. Since it appeared on the educational scene in the late 1980s, character education has gained the support of many persons concerned with the education of children, including teachers, parents, business leaders, and government. More and more schools are incorporating character-related curriculum into their instruction and character-related expectations into their school climate.

The results have been impressive. Teachers report an improved learning environment, with fewer discipline problems and a more pleasant classroom atmosphere. School administrators report improved relationships with parents, better attendance, fewer problems with both students and staff, and—that most important of results—improved test scores. Parents relate that their children have better attitudes at home, are better members of their communities, and often become better students. Business and civic leaders are typically delighted with a emphasis on character in their communities because they know that the students of today are the citizens and workforce of tomorrow. Character education is making a difference in many schools.

The character education movement began in the elementary grades but quickly spread to include middle grades, high schools, and even colleges. Impressive results were seen when character education was taught in elementary schools, and teachers of older children began to think

> **Why begin character education in the later grades?**
>
> We can't afford to miss even one student with the lessons of good character.

that their classrooms could be improved as well. Knowing that middle- and high-school students would soon be entering the workforce, it seemed all the more imperative to try to reach them, too, with character education.

Initially dismissed by some as a fad, character education seems to have settled into the U.S. educational scene. Teachers and administrators accustomed to including character education in their curriculum cannot imagine their schools without it. The methods of character education are slowly being proven by nearly a decade of experience in classrooms. Increasing numbers of communities are calling for schools to do more to curb violence, improve learning, and teach basic civic principles to students. Perhaps the greatest indication of its promise as a force in effective education is the inclusion of character education curriculum in teacher training programs at a growing number of universities.

As of late 2000, the following states have received federal funding for character education programs: Alabama, California, Colorado, Connecticut, Georgia, Hawaii, Illinois, Indiana, Iowa, Kansas, Kentucky, Maryland, Minnesota, Mississippi, New Hampshire, New Jersey, New Mexico, New York, North Carolina, North Dakota, Ohio, Oklahoma, Oregon, Pennsylvania, South Carolina, Utah, Washington, and Wisconsin. Many states have provided additional funding from their own treasuries as well.

In character education, as in many things, the best teacher will be your own experience. Not everyone in your school will be as enthusiastic as you might hope. Some people are inspired by ideas, and others are

Eleven Basic Principles from The Character Education Partnership

When starting out in the field of character education, it's helpful to learn from those who have been pioneers in this area. One of the first places to start is with resources from The Character Education Partnership (CEP). CEP is a nonprofit and nonpartisan coalition of organizations and individuals dedicated to promoting character. A great deal of information and resources can be found on their Web site (http://www.character.org/) and in their printed materials. Three leaders in character education (Tom Lickona, Eric Schaps, and Catherine Lewis) have authored the CEP document entitled "Eleven Principles of Effective Character Education." Persons who are new to character education will benefit from reading the full text of this publication (see Resource Guide).

Eleven Principles of Effective Character Education™

1. Character education promotes core ethical values as the basis of good character.
2. "Character" must be comprehensively defined to include thinking, feeling, and behavior.
3. Effective character education requires an intentional, proactive, and comprehensive approach that promotes the core values in all phases of school life.
4. The school must be a caring community.
5. To develop character, students need opportunities for moral action.
6. Effective character education includes a meaningful and challenging academic curriculum that respects all learners and helps them succeed.
7. Character education should strive to develop students' intrinsic motivation.
8. The school staff must become a learning and moral community in which all share responsibility for character education and attempt to adhere to the same core values that guide the education of students.
9. Character education requires moral leadership from both staff and students.
10. The school must recruit parents and community members as full partners in the character-building effort.
11. Evaluation of character education should assess the character of the school, the school staff's functioning as character educators, and the extent to which students manifest good character.

Used with permission.

> Some people are inspired by ideas.
>
> Others are inspired by results.

inspired by results. Those persons who find themselves "on fire" with the potential of an idea may have to carry the program until it starts yielding results. When things start changing at your school, however, you'll probably start seeing others lending their support to the initiative.

As you embark on a program of character education in your school, take your time the first year. Keep moving, but try not to push things on people. The proof, as they say, is in the pudding: a dynamic and effective character education program will prove itself in the lives of students and in the climate of the school. Most teachers chose this profession because they wanted to make a difference in the lives of students. Seeing that difference will eventually quell any dissent from teachers who didn't think formal character education was needed.

Good character is taught; it is not innate. It is taught by modeling, by instruction, and by interactions with people who are important in the daily lives of students. It really matters little what method you use to teach character as long as you are aware of the example you are setting, are deliberately teaching character, and are cognizant of the interactions between didactic teaching and real-world learning. Today's students need healthy role models and positive things to be committed to. Above all, they need leadership—someone to show them the way toward adulthood. Implementing a character program is a wonderful opportunity to share with the world your optimism and your belief in the ability of teachers to influence children's lives for the better.

Dream Big

If there were ever a time to dare to make a difference,
To embark on something worth doing,
It is now.

Not for any grand cause necessarily,
But for something that tugs at your heart,
Something that's your aspiration,
Something that's your dream.

You owe it to yourself to make your days here count.
Have fun.
Dig deep.
Stretch.
Dream big.

Know, though, that things worth doing seldom come easy.
There will be good days
And there will be bad days.
There will be times when you want to turn around,
Pack it up, and call it quits.

Those times tell you
That you are pushing yourself,
That you are not afraid to learn by trying.
Persist.

Because with an idea, determination, and the right tools,
You can do great things.
Let your instincts, your intellect, and your heart guide you.
Trust.

Believe in the incredible power of the human mind,
Of doing something that makes a difference,
Of working hard,
Of laughing and hoping,
Of lazy afternoons,
Of lasting friends,
Of all the things that will cross your path this year.

The start of something new brings the hope of something great.
Anything is possible.
There is only one you,
And you will pass this way only once.
Do it right!

Author Unknown

Character education is gaining momentum as a powerful and positive force in the schooling of children.

Chapter 2

Getting Started in Character Education

"All glory comes from daring to begin."
—Eugene F. Ware

If you are new to character education, getting started can feel over-whelming even as it feels exciting. What do you do first? Second? Third? As with any new venture, the best place to start is with your own preparation. By researching the subject and figuring out logistical details, you can help the initial committee meetings run more smoothly. You'll also need to establish a group of people who will help carry out the program's implementation—this is not something one person can accomplish on his or her own. Establishing the character committee and getting support from the administration are key parts of beginning a program. A final component of getting started is to explore your role as committee chairperson. How will you lead the program?

Doing Your Homework

One of the first steps in getting started is to prepare yourself, to "do your homework." A good place to begin is to read what you can on the subject. Several helpful books are available describing the theory and history of character education and providing examples of its successful implementation in schools. A number of character-related organizations have formed around the movement, and they usually have literature available. Some states have their own clearinghouses of character-related information, particularly those states with large federal grants or man-dated character programs. Numerous resources are available through the Internet as well. For a list of suggested materials and Web sites, see the Resource Guide. As you read, take time to gather copies of pertinent materials to share with members of the character committee at your first meeting.

Another part of doing your homework is to find out some details about the proposed character program at your school. You'll want to investigate several issues before you go into the first committee meeting. Use the following questions as a guide:

- Is there funding available for the program? If so, how much of it is available to the committee? What are the restrictions on how the funding is to be used?

- What kinds of resources are available to the committee? Is there a district-wide coordinator who could provide assistance or materials?

- Who or what is driving the implementation of character education in your school? Is it resulting from a district- or state-wide mandate?

- How much authority does the committee have in determining the particulars of the program? Are you being provided with a pre-written program that you are expected to implement or will you create your own program?

- Is there a school nearby that could serve as a model for your program?

Getting started in character education involves:

- Doing your homework

- Setting up the committee

- Understanding your role as leader

You will undoubtedly learn more about these points as you gain experience. Don't wait to start until you've got it all figured out.

- How does your school administration feel about the character education program? Are they fully supportive of its implementation?

Setting Up the Committee

A key step in getting started is to establish the character committee. Because the program will succeed or not based on the people involved, it's important that members of the committee:

- **Be persons of good character.** The program will have greater credibility if committee members consistently model good character.

- **Believe in the program.** To gain support for the program throughout the school, members of the committee must be advocates for character education.

- **Be willing to work hard to ensure its success.** Much work is involved in establishing an effective program. Committee members should be willing to assume responsibility for tasks and be dependable to follow through.

Suggestions for assembling an effective committee

Ask for volunteers
Asking for volunteers may seem risky (after all, you could get someone you'd rather avoid), but it's not good for the program if

Questions to answer

✔ Funding available?

✔ Who's driving this?

✔ Type of program?

✔ District models?

✔ Support of administration?

people think they aren't welcome on the committee. If possible, you'll want to avoid negative persons and those who are unwilling to listen to others' ideas. However, if such a person is interested in being on the committee, accept him or her gracefully. It could be that the committee is just what this person needs to stretch and grow.

Hold an annual staff review

At least once per year, hold a forum on character education that every staff member is invited to attend. This is an opportunity to discuss the value of the character education program in the school, to get new ideas regarding the program, and to solicit feedback on perceived problems with the program. It's also a good time to recruit new committee members. As new teachers join the school staff, be sure to encourage their interest in the committee. Getting new staff on board early is a plus for the program.

Recruit the go-getters

It's been said that, in any group of people, 1/3 of the people are go-getters, 1/3 are fence-sitters, and 1/3 do only what is required. It takes a lot of work and initiative to have an effective program, so you will want to recruit those "go-getters" for the committee. Actively recruit staff members who express interest in the committee, who are key to the school leadership, who work hard, who are popular role models with students, and who seem to do well on teams. Keep your eyes open for people who might be assets to the character committee, and personally invite them to join. Don't wait for them to come to you—some people want to be asked.

Seek representation from core departments

It's ideal to have a representative on the committee from each core department in the school. This is a key element in getting everyone in the school to support the tenets of the character program, and it will help keep department members aware of the committee's plans. It's also helpful to involve people such as sports coaches or other activity directors, as they have opportunities to reinforce the character teachings outside of the school day.

Pay attention to diversity

The character education committee should reflect the diversity of your school staff. If your school is culturally diverse, you can avoid many problems by making sure that different ethnic and cultural backgrounds are represented on the committee. This diversity will help prevent polarization of different staff groups against the efforts of the committee, and it will also help you gain support from parents and others in the community. Do your best to ensure that the group is balanced in terms of gender.

Include an administrator

It's imperative that the character education program have full support from the school administration. Your school's principal is critical to success and must be kept informed of the committee's plans, though it is not always possible for him or her to be directly involved. It helps to have at least one administrator (i.e., principal or assistant principal) in each meeting because this person can help you with certain logistics. The administrator is likely to know how to set up a special program, how to arrange field trips, and how to

Recruit committee members who:

- Have positive attitudes

- Are honest and trustworthy

- Are dependable

- Take responsibility

- Care about the school

- Listen well and communicate effectively

- Are decision-makers

- Are willing to learn and grow

Success Tip: Try to limit the committee to about 8-10 persons. The larger your committee, the more difficult it is to conduct meetings effectively. If your school is very large, you might want to have a larger committee with active sub-committees. However, you're probably better off starting with fewer people and involving others as needed for particular projects.

handle other administrative issues. Furthermore, the administrator's involvement subtly encourages the program by making it clear that he or she is behind the effort. Don't expect the administrator to assume a leadership role in accomplishing the work of the committee, though; administrators usually have other responsibilities that claim their time.

You may find it helpful to prepare a handout that explains the role of the character education committee. This may be hard to develop the first year, but after that you'll have a pretty good idea of what new members can expect. The handout should cover topics such as meeting time and frequency, compensation (if any), and activities supported by the committee. Also, you might include a list of committee roles, the mission statement, and an overview of the committee's efforts to date.

Be sure administrators are involved

One point bears repeating: it is extremely important to involve school administrators in the character education program. Administrators—including the principal, assistant principals, and guidance counselors—set the tone for the whole school. They have many opportunities to champion the character effort in the school while performing their usual tasks, such as evaluating and encouraging staff members, dealing with individual parents and students, and working with personnel from the school system's central office.

The principal is the lead teacher in the school and a key character model. He or she will lead the staff by example, whether positive or negative. The principal has a pivotal role in enlisting staff support and providing the time and resources necessary for the program. The principal also needs to be a cheerleader for the committee; because the efforts of the character education committee may be intensely scrutinized, committee members in particular need to receive positive reinforcement.

Assistant principals are typically the ones who handle discipline problems, so they too have a vital role in reinforcing character traits with students and with parents. Furthermore, assistant principals are more likely than teachers to have one-on-one time with students, particularly those students most in need of character education. Similarly, the guidance staff have daily opportunities to reinforce character lessons with individual students. These staff members can help students apply character lessons to their unique situations—an invaluable extension of the school-wide program.

Being A Leader

A final thing to get a handle on as you embark on a character education program is your role as committee chairperson. As the leader of this effort, you are in the hot seat. Ultimately, it is by your sweat and charisma that the program moves forward. Granted, you need support from the school administration and staff for the program to be effective. You also need the help and cooperation of other committee members. But it is the chair of the committee, more than any other person, who shepherds the program. As chairperson, you should be able to answer "Yes" to the following questions.

Chairperson

✓ Visionary

✓ Negotiator

✓ Cheerleader

✓ Challenger

✓ Grunt

Dealing with criticism

You won't win any popularity contests for being involved with the character education committee, no matter how hard you work. In fact, it may be just the opposite. Because committee members are the chief "modelers" of character for the school, they may find that their own character is criticized by other teachers and by students. Don't allow yourself to feel attacked. Be prepared for criticism, and try to remain enthusiastic about the program. As the committee receives critical feedback, weigh each comment and decide if changes are needed. Discuss how others in the school are perceiving you as a group. Help committee members remain vigilant about the task of sharing and modeling good character.

Q: Are you willing to consistently exhibit good character?
In this role, you will be challenged continuously to model good character. As the character education chairperson, you will have the opportunity to examine your own life, and you will become keenly aware of your own set of ethics. Commit yourself to living consistently and honestly. You really will have to lead by example.

Q: Can you respect and work with all types of people?
If you have biases and prejudices, they will invariably show up in your committee leadership. You need to be respectful of everyone's contribution and be able to see the value that each member brings to the committee—even a stubborn member who seems to slow everything down. Because personal conflicts will destroy a committee, you must be able to leave personal preferences out of your professional interactions. Your body language is important in this regard: your face or posture can be a sure give-away of how you feel about a topic (or a person).

Q: Do you have a good relationship with the school administration?
The committee chairperson absolutely must have a good relationship with the administration. If you are continually locking horns with administrators, your program will go nowhere. The character committee needs their support, and you must be able to talk to them easily. Their involvement is critical.

Q: Do you have time to give?
Running an effective character education program requires a great deal of extra-curricular work. This work can be very rewarding,

creative, and satisfying, but it will take time away from other things in your life. You will probably be called on to:

- Meet with business partners
- Help prepare grants
- Meet with persons interested in your program
- Be interviewed by the press
- Work with other schools
- Share the story of what is happening at your school

These tasks can add up to as much as 10-20 hours per week. You have to be willing to give that time without resentment. Furthermore, if a committee member does not follow through on a commitment, you may have to pick up the pieces and finish the task yourself. Be prepared to give extra. Along with the time demands, however, you have the opportunity to make a real difference.

Q: Can you handle conflict effectively?

Being a good leader means you have a responsibility to watch out for the group as a whole, for the program, and for the atmosphere created in the meetings. Handling conflict is part of being a leader, and you should be able to handle conflict calmly and effectively. As the committee chairperson, you will have to stay on top of all the committee plans and follow up as necessary. You may have to prod team members to do their agreed-upon tasks. This can be challenging and uncomfortable, and it is inevitable that someone will be upset with you. If your primary goal is to ensure that everyone likes you, it will lead to mediocrity and ineffectiveness. A good

Success Tip: You should constantly stress to committee members that "this is our committee, not my committee." Watch out that you don't expect it to become "your" committee.

leader must sometimes make difficult and unpopular decisions in order to to keep the progran moving forward.

Q: Can you take the heat?

As the committee chairperson, you may be ostracized by some staff members. You may be seen as an ally of the administration, particularly if the principal is a strong proponent of the character education program, and you may be mistrusted by other teachers. Furthermore, some teachers may be jealous of you. You are likely to be busy with the committee's projects and plans, and you may be asked to represent the school at outside functions. This opportunity to be out of the building may be seen by some as a bonus, even though to you it may represent a great deal of extra work. Occasionally, you will encounter critics who resent you and what you represent; examine yourself to see if there is something you can improve upon, but don't be overly worried about them. Finally, when something goes wrong with the program, even if it's not your fault, you will probably be accountable for the issue. This is what we mean by "taking the heat."

Should the role of committee chair be rotated?

Some persons may suggest that the role of committee chairperson be rotated, but this is probably not a good idea for a character education committee. For the integrity of the program, it is essential that one person in the school is in charge of the program. A single person, rather than several, will help ensure consistency in the character program. This person will have an overall view of the different program components and will be able to make decisions if necessary. In some situations you may need another person to lead a meeting, but that is different from being in charge of the entire program. In fact, it's a good idea to identify an assistant or co-chairperson to help deal with some of the issues that arise and to provide leadership when you are absent.

It's always healthy for the program to think ahead to when you or a co-chairperson might move or be transferred to another school. Encourage the committee to develop into a core group of people who are jointly driving the character initiative. If the program is driven primarily by one focal leader, the initiative may die if that person leaves the school.

Defining your role

By taking on the role of character committee chairperson, you're indicating a willingness to be a leader. One of the biggest challenges you may face in establishing the committee is to clearly define your role as chairperson. As the leader, you must provide both direction and support to help the committee accomplish its goals. In most cases, though, this role will be complicated by two issues:

1. You are likely to be a peer of your committee members, not their supervisor.
2. The committee's efforts are probably voluntary.

Thus, traditional methods used by supervisors to motivate employees won't work. You have to find a new way to operate.

Leadership is really the efforts of one person to influence the behavior of another person. When you lead, you do so because of some power or influence which gives you authority. You are not a leader if nobody follows! As the chairperson of a committee comprised of peer volunteers, you have three basic ways to earn the distinction of "leader":

- By your expertise,
- By your charisma, and/or
- By your ability to get things done.

Power of expertise

From time to time, we agree to follow the leadership of someone based on their expertise. For example, we usually follow the advice of a doctor when we are ill, and we listen to our accountant for tax advice. In education, people will follow the leadership of peers and staff specialists who have proven that they "know their stuff."

Power of charisma

Some persons become leaders because of their dynamic, charismatic personalities. This is frequently seen in politicians, activists, and spiritual leaders, for example. In education, we all know the teacher who can take on a task enthusiastically, encourage others to participate, and see the task through to completion with confidence and skill. You may be this kind of person, and if so, leadership probably comes easily to you.

Power of hard work

Some persons are natural leaders because of their tireless ability to get things done. As the committee gains a reputation for its accomplishments, your reputation as a leader will increase as well. It is your job as committee chairperson to seek out and remove the obstacles that keep the committee from being effective. You may have to run interference with the central board office. You may have to deal with irate parents. You may have to bring disparate groups of people together. You may have to stay up late stuffing envelopes or folding newsletters. All of these are part of the job.

Your behavior will naturally follow your values and principles. If you espouse one value but act out another, you will quickly lose credibility among your committee members. As the leader, then, you have certain responsibilities toward your committee members such as:

- **Championing the committee's vision, mission, and goals.** You are the chief cheerleader. Thus, you should support both the program and the committee members in all situations.

- **Treating everyone with respect, as you would want to be treated.** This means respecting individuals' contributions to the committee, being courteous, fair, and respectful, and soliciting their input on issues.

- **Being open and honest in your communications.** The character committee does not exist in a vacuum; it is interdependent with all the other organizations in the school. For this reason, good communication should be a high priority. Why not be the one to initiate conversations with the leaders of other

What are your expectations?

Our effectiveness as leaders begins with our expectations. What you expect of the committee can be very powerful in influencing its success. For years physicians have known about the placebo effect: that some sick people will get better when they take medicine they believe will cure them, even if unknowingly they are taking a sugar pill. With that in mind, resist the tendency to treat a committee member as a "problem" based on a past experience with that person.

The lesson of self-fulfilling prophecies is this: if you believe something is true, and act on it as true, then whether it is true or not, you will help it come about. This principle holds in medicine, in business, and even in education. You get what you expect to get. Having an effective committee begins with expecting that the members are a world-class group of people who want to do an excellent job. If you think anything less than that, you will set in motion a downward spiral of disappointment, lowered expectations, and more disappointment.

groups to resolve conflicts and to head off problems before they happen?

- **Working with peers collaboratively toward a common goal.** Working together to reach consensus means that all members—including the chairperson—must be willing to compromise. Sometimes this can be very hard to do, especially when you don't think a particular idea will be effective. You cannot have your own agenda and expect the committee to carry it out.

Your role as challenger

There is one last area of being a leader that shouldn't be overlooked. You may be a terrific organizer, a hard worker, and an inspiration, but how good are you at confronting someone who is not doing his or her share of the work? The role of challenger can be a very difficult one to assume, yet few things are as demoralizing to a team as one person who is not "pulling their weight." As a leader, it is your responsibility to identify problems (or potential problems) in the committee and challenge committee members when necessary. Some tips on this role include:

- **Be sure that the committee's expectations are understood.** This is particularly important for persons who are new to the committee. They may not know what you expect and may be operating from a "best guess" based on the last group they were involved with. Your expectations may be surprising to them, so it is best that they understand the committee's standards up front. If you wait until you are fuming to state what's expected, you risk angering and discouraging the person.

- **Be specific.** When challenging a committee member, be specific about what you want to see happen. By being specific, you can often mitigate the person's resistance or defensiveness. Compare these two requests:
    1. "Barbara, will you distribute the minutes?"
    2. "Barbara, will you make sure that the minutes are distributed by noon tomorrow so everyone knows what they are responsible for next week?"

- **Focus on problem-solving, not problems.** You'll be more successful if you don't dwell on why a problem occurred, but focus instead on how it can be resolved. Excuses are typically our first response to a problem, and they often lead to debate over the facts, escalating emotions, and no real resolution. Skip that part, and focus instead on how the problem can be prevented from happening in the future.

Because the leader of the character committee is often on display, your faults may be quickly pointed out. Ultimately, you will lead by example. Nothing sums this up better than the following poem, adapted to fit the teacher:

Lessons We See

I would rather see a lesson than hear one any day.

I would rather one should walk with me than merely show the
way.

The eye's a better pupil, and more willing than the ear;

Fine counsel is confusing, but example is always clear.

The best of all the teachers are the ones who live their creeds,

For to see the good in action is what everybody needs.

I can soon learn how to do it, if you will let me see it done;

I can watch your hands in action, but your tongue too fast may
run.

The lectures you deliver may be very wise and true,

But I would rather get my lesson by observing what you do.

For I may misunderstand you and the high advice you give,

But there is no misunderstanding

How you act and how you live!

Author Unknown

Covey on Leadership

In *Principle-Centered Leadership* (Simon and Schuster, 1992), Dr. Stephen Covey emphasizes the need for win-win agreements. Leaders must communicate the vision of the committee, live its key principles in their day-to-day responsibilities, and inspire others to do the same, Covey says. The following are characteristics Covey uses to describe principle-centered leaders:

- **They are continually learning**—Expanding their knowledge, competence, and skills through training, talking with others, and experience.

- **They are service-oriented**—Thinking of the needs of others and acting accordingly.

- **They radiate positive energy**—Using their spirits to inspire others.

- **They believe in people**—Believing in unseen potential and creating a climate where others can grow.

- **They lead balanced lives**—Giving attention to all areas of their lives.

- **They see life as an adventure**—Exploring new ideas and being ready to challenge the status quo.

- **They are synergistic**—Building on their strengths and seeking out others to help with their liabilities.

- **They exercise for self-renewal**—Exercising physical, mental, and emotional dimensions.

As you embark upon this journey, realize that you have the skills within yourself to make it successful.

Chapter 3

The First Meetings

"Interest = Energy; Organization = Time"
—Wolfgang Lederer

No one enjoys a meeting where much is said but nothing is accomplished, where the group goes around and around an issue but never finds resolution. When we leave an effective meeting, however, we're satisfied that our time was invested well, and we're motivated to do the tasks we've agreed to do. Well-run meetings can contribute immensely to how people feel about serving on the character committee.

Planning the Initial Meeting

The first meeting of the school year sets the tone for the rest of the committee meetings. It is very important to be well-organized for this meeting, because this is where you begin to establish group norms—the unwritten code of behavior that committee members will follow. Allow at least an hour for the first meeting. If possible, schedule it during the teacher work days before classes begin. After the committee is established, you may want to hold the first meeting of subsequent school years at your home and serve lunch. This starts the committee off on a personal note, allowing time to socialize as well as plan for the upcoming year.

The initial meeting of any new committee is a time to get organized and become familiar with each other. You'll want to use this meeting to get acquainted, to decide how you will operate as a committee, and to discuss your overall goals for the year. Your leadership style at this meeting will let committee members know what they can expect from you. Are you

Success Tip: Begin the meetings on time, even if only half of the committee has arrived. Then end on time as well, even if you don't get through your agenda. You are setting the expectation that the meetings will start and end on time. Adhering to time limits is to your benefit: people are more willing to attend meetings if they can depend on them to end at a certain time, and they will be less likely to digress during the meeting itself.

going to make all the decisions? Or, are you going to express your opinions but not dominate the discussion? As the leader, you need to set the direction, get everyone involved, and then back away—while making sure that all members are heard. As you might imagine, this is no small task!

An effective first meeting begins with your preparation. The meeting will run more smoothly if you can get to the room early and have everything set up before people start arriving. Before the meeting:

- Arrange the chairs or desks in a circle.
- Prepare refreshments for people to enjoy as they come in.
- Place the handouts you have prepared at each person's seat.

Here are some suggestions on how to structure the first meeting:

1. Begin with introductions. Introduce yourself and go over the meeting agenda. Then ask the members to introduce themselves, share their visions for the committee (or why they want to be involved), and state what unique skill or characteristic they are bringing to the group. Try to keep this light-hearted and fun.

2. Ask for a volunteer to take notes during the meeting and to distribute those notes to committee members the following day. At each transition point, ask the note-taker to summarize his or her notes on the preceding discussion.

3. Provide an overview of the tasks of the committee. One approach is to begin with a statement such as, "Our committee

has the unique opportunity to define for our school what a character education program is all about, and then to elicit the support we need to do that job and to do it well." It will help if you have this statement written on a chalkboard or flip chart in advance of the meeting. Another approach is to begin with a short story, poem, or testimonial of how the environment at a particular school has been transformed with a character education program. Allow some time for committee members to reach agreement on their tasks, but don't get bogged down (yet!) in defining the particulars of how you will accomplish them.

4. Explain how you plan to operate as chairperson, what you expect from the committee, and what they can expect from you. This is where you can discuss the importance of consensus, for example. Emphasize that this is "our" committee, rather than "your" committee. Also, explain the different roles that will be needed and how the roles will be rotated weekly. At the least, you will need someone to take and distribute the meeting notes, someone to write on the flip chart, and someone to watch the time. By rotating the different roles, responsibility is shared among all committee members. Finally, point out that committee members must work together to make character education a success. If people leave the meeting and voice their criticisms to others, it tears the committee down. Thus, problematic issues need to be discussed in the meeting, not with outsiders.

> ## Goals for the first meeting
>
> ✔ Get to know each other
>
> ✔ Agree on your mission
>
> ✔ Set ground rules
>
> ✔ Identify key program components

5. Develop a mission statement, which is a clear statement of why your committee exists. Your mission statement should include the purpose of your committee, the primary persons affected by your purpose, and the primary means by which you intend to fulfill this purpose. Put this mission statement at the top of all newsletters, memos, and other information distributed by you or the committee.

6. Establish the ground rules. These are simply agreements on how you will operate as a committee, addressing issues such as: Will you require consensus? What kind of support is expected from the team? You may want to brainstorm the rules of the committee first, then discuss each idea. (Refer to the discussion on brainstorming later in this chapter.) Combine any similar items and make a short list of your committee rules on how you are going to proceed together. You may want to ask everyone to sign the list, or have the recorder note in the minutes that the committee is in agreement on the ground rules.

7. Establish when and how often the committee will meet. It is helpful to schedule your meetings for the entire school year at the beginning of the year. Choose a day that is easy to remember, such as the first and third Tuesdays of the month, or the Monday following your monthly staff meeting. Make sure your meetings are listed on the school calendar. Keep the meeting room in the same place if at all possible to help eliminate confusion.

Sample mission statement

Our mission is to promote good character in our school. To do this we will plan, implement, and encourage activities that teach and reinforce positive character traits among our students.

8. Brainstorm ways in which character education can be most effective in your school. What will be the key components of the program? What can you do first? What should be done second?

9. Decide which components will form the core of your program for the year. You may want to use a decision-making tool such as multi-voting at this point. (Refer to the following discussion of techniques.)

10. If time allows, establish a tentative master plan. Type up the plan after the meeting and give copies to the committee members to review. Ask them to think about the plan and be ready to discuss it again at the next meeting. It is very important to reach a consensus on the approach you are taking with the program so that everyone will give it their full support. If necessary, spend another meeting working toward consensus on this issue; it will greatly enhance your overall effectiveness.

11. End by setting the agenda for the next meeting.

12. Ask a committee member to provide feedback to the group on how the meeting went. Praise them for discussions that went well, and thank them for listening to each other.

In the days following the first meeting, try to touch base with the committee members individually to ask them what they thought of the meeting. After attending the first meeting, some persons may decide

---

Sample ground rules

- Begin and end on time

- Do not interrupt

- One conversation at a time

- Remain open-minded

- Follow the agenda

- Maintain confidentiality

- Support committee decisions

- Provide positive feedback to committee members

that they do not want to be involved with the committee. If this happens, don't take it personally. It doesn't matter what their reasons are. Allow them to exit gracefully.

Running Effective Meetings

In the business world, tremendous amounts of time and money are invested in training employees on how to have effective meetings; businesses know that such training can help their companies be more profitable by making the most of employees' time. In education, unfortunately, almost no one is trained in how to run effective meetings. You can help the committee function more smoothly and effectively by adapting tools commonly used in meetings conducted at well-run businesses.

Meeting tools

Agendas

Agendas are an essential tool for effective meetings. When creating an agenda, list the topics in the order they will be discussed. It's helpful to list the more important items toward the top—if you run out of time, you will have covered the critical items. Having an outline of what will be discussed and in what order helps focus the group and reduces digressions. Make it a habit to distribute the agenda in advance of each meeting so that committee members can prepare. An agenda distributed on the morning of the meeting also helps remind everyone of the meeting that day. Similarly, when the committee is holding a special program, such as an assembly or

Sample Action Agenda

Priority	Item	Accountability	Timing
1	Make banners	Joan, Todd	Aug. 30th
2	Make posters	Steve	Sept. 5th
3	Plan parent night activities	Janet, Marco	Sept. 12th
4	Decide on an assembly speaker, schedule	Joan, Chin	Sept. 15th
5	Develop a resource notebook for teachers	Steve, Annette	Sept. 19th

other event, use an agenda format to outline the event. Be sure that committee members have this information in advance of other staff members so they can answer questions if needed.

A variation of the typical list-type agenda is an *action agenda*. This sort of agenda is helpful in pinning down priorities and account-abilities. To create an action agenda, develop a table with four columns, as shown above. The first column contains the priority of the item (1st, 2nd, 3rd, etc.). The second column lists the action item or project, and the third column identifies who is responsible for the item. The fourth column contains information on timing. The action agenda can be used as your meeting agenda, if your committee is very task-oriented, or it can be included in the minutes to remind everyone of the status of key projects. If you use this tool, remember to update the action agenda at every meeting.

Minutes

Ask someone on the committee to be responsible for taking meeting notes (also called minutes) and for distributing them to members in a timely fashion. Unless absolutely necessary, don't take on this task yourself—let someone else handle it. If an item that is not on the agenda comes up during a meeting, ask the recorder to note it in the minutes so it can be discussed at a later time.

Visual aids

It might seem obvious, particularly to teachers, that visual aids are a tremendous help in focusing attention. Don't forget to use visual aids in your committee meetings as well. Plan to have a flip chart or chalkboard in your meeting room so it can be used as needed. When you fill the flip chart page with notes, post it on the wall; this way everyone can continue to see the notes even as you move on to another sheet. Using visual aids will help keep everyone's heads looking up instead of down, so you will be able to read facial expressions and body language more easily.

Timelines

Reach consensus on a timeline for each project you are going to sponsor, and include the timeline in the meeting minutes. If your committee is using funds from grants supporting character education, you will become familiar with setting timelines and being expected to meet them; this is an important component of grant funding.

Useful techniques

Several techniques commonly used by business teams can help the committee generate new ideas and make decisions. Using these techniques can increase your efficiency and help meetings run more smoothly.

Brainstorming

During a brainstorming session, committee members are invited to suggest ideas related to the topic at hand. The ideas are written down in front of the group on a large flipchart or chalkboard. It's important not to discuss or comment on the ideas when they are listed, as this can inhibit creativity. Use the *round-robin technique* to encourage everyone's participation: go around the group in sequence, with each person throwing out only one idea per turn.

Success Tip: Keep in mind that some members may not know how to take charge and get things done. You may need to coach them on how to move forward with their tasks. This can be challenging for you, but being friendly and helpful is important; view it as helping the person to develop leadership skills.

Multi-voting

This tool can help with decision-making when there are numerous options available and only a few can be chosen—for example, when you are deciding among several traits or projects, or when only a few students are needed for a project and many are interested in participating. Everyone on the team is given the same number of votes (10, for example), and each person casts those votes for their top choices. From the tally, the group's top choices are usually apparent. It's often helpful to use a "10/4 guideline": everyone gets ten votes and can put a maximum of four votes on any one choice.

Storyboarding

This variation of multi-voting relies on the visual display of information. There are two ways to set up a storyboard:

1. Place drafting tape sticky-side up in long vertical strips. Give everyone a stack of index cards and a marker. (Drafting tape is important because you can pull the cards off and move them around easily.)

2. Tape several pieces of flip-chart paper to a nearby wall. Give everyone a stack of large Post-it® notes and a marker.

Next, take a few minutes for each person to write down as many ideas related to the topic as they can, one idea per card or Post-it® note. Collect these ideas and place them on the strips of tape or flip-chart paper, eliminating duplicates as you go along. As cate-

---

Brainstorming

Used to help generate ideas about a particular topic. Example: What's the most effective way to engage parents in our school's character program?

Multi-voting

Used to help the group make a decision among several choices. Example: Which six (or ten, or twenty) character traits will we emphasize this year?

Storyboarding

Used to categorize different ideas and reach consensus about which categories to pursue first. Example: What activities and programs will be part of our character initiative this year?

Success Tip: Develop a meeting kit that you bring to every meeting. Find a medium-sized tote with a handle and fill it with all the supplies you might need during a meeting. Include chalk and chart markers; spare paper and pens; drafting tape, index cards, Post-It® notes, and dots (for storyboarding); and hard candies or other treats. With a meeting kit, you will always have the tools you need readily available. You won't waste meeting time searching for a chart marker!

gories become apparent, group the related cards together on a single strip of tape or page and write a header card, preferably in red marker. When all the ideas are "on the wall," give each member the same number of red or orange "dot" stickers, available at any school supply store, and let them place their stickers on the cards or categories that they feel are most important. When you step back and look at your storyboard, you will see a visual display of the group's choices.

Facilitating the Group

As chairperson, it is your job to keep the group on task. When there is a diversion, allow only a very short discussion before suggesting that the item be "parked" on the agenda for later. As soon as possible, you might say to the group something like, "I agree with you that this is an important point, but for the sake of time, let's refocus on the items on today's agenda." Another suggestion is, "We all want to know the answer to that, but this is not the time to talk about it. Let's focus on the agenda so that we can finish on time." In some cases you may want to structure the meeting so that an anticipated diversion is postponed until the end of the meeting.

With experience, you'll learn to read the body language of committee members and to draw them into the conversation accordingly. For example, you might notice that a certain member is looking down with pursed lips. You could say, "John, it looks like you don't agree with this direction. What are your feelings on the issue?" As much as possible, encourage everyone's full participation.

Reaching consensus

It's also your job to establish consensus-based decision-making as the norm. When a committee reaches consensus, it means that all members have reached an agreement they can support. This support is critical to your success. Voting, on the other hand, results in decisions made by part of the committee—and therefore supported only by part of the committee. Voting can also create hard feelings and divisions among members.

If the committee is unable to reach consensus on an issue, don't panic. Try to view disagreement as healthy and keep it positive rather than negative. If the group is deadlocked on a particular issue, you might try one of the following techniques to encourage discussion. Most groups can eventually reach a consensus.

- **Describe the pros and cons of the issue.** On a large piece of paper or chalkboard, list the pros and cons of both positions. Then challenge the members to think of another option that addresses both positions.

- **Table the issue.** Set the issue aside until the next meeting if you can. In most cases, consensus can be reached more easily after some time has elapsed. Put it first on the agenda at your next meeting. If time is short, you may need to call a special meeting at a later date. This gives everyone a chance to reflect on the issue and perhaps gain a different perspective.

Character Survival Kits

At some point during the year, it can be fun to give teachers and staff "Character Survival Kits." Simply fill small bags with the following items and give one to each person, along with a note explaining the reasons for the contents. Alternately, you could give a "survival kit" to all the character committee members.

Item	Character Reminder
Chocolate Kiss	To show love and kindness to one another
Candle	To light up the school with a positive attitude
Band-Aid	To help heal hurt feelings (either our own or someone else's)
Button	To "button our lips" to keep from saying unkind words
Toothpick	To pick out the good qualities in others
Eraser	To erase others' mistakes
Sticker	To stick together as a team
Mint	To remember that we're worth a mint to each other
Lifesaver	To seek each other out when we need someone to talk to

An effective committee is a cornerstone of success with character education.

Chapter

Choosing Your Teaching Approach

"Intelligence, plus character, that is the goal of true education."
—*Dr. Martin Luther King, Jr.*

There's no right or wrong way to approach character education. The most important question to ask is: "What approach will work best in our school?" How you will teach character and which traits you will emphasize are among the first decisions the committee will make.

Regardless of the specific approach you take, two attitudes can help the character program be most effective: modeling good character and taking advantage of teachable moments throughout the day. These components of the program require no preparation—instead, they require the awareness and willingness of individual teachers.

The most effective way to teach good character is to model it. Students will be watching your actions to see whether you really believe in the concepts you are teaching. Children are very good at pointing out your inconsistencies, and they will be the first to tell you when you are not demonstrating good character. This doesn't mean that you can't get upset, or that you have to be perfect—it simply means that regularly and routinely you must practice traits which demonstrate good character with everyone in the school building. Students observe and learn from how staff members treat each other. Do you talk about the school administrators in front of students? Do you allow students to discuss administrators and other teachers in your classroom? What is your attitude toward custodians and secretaries? If you don't "practice what you preach," chances are good your students will figure that out.

Modeling is the primary way students learn character.

Good character also can be taught very effectively by taking advantage of "teachable moments." These are opportunities during the day when you can casually and matter-of-factly emphasize "right choices." As your students read stories, write, work on computers, or do math, look for ways to comment on good character. Don't limit yourself to events occurring in your classroom; if students are discussing something that happened outside the classroom, take up the issue briefly and help them reframe the situation in terms of character. A few minutes of specific application can drive a lesson home more effectively than hours of formal instruction.

Selecting a School-Wide Approach

To institute a formal program in character education, you will probably decide on a school-wide approach for including character education in your curriculum. Several different approaches have been used effectively. Saturation teaching, in which the lessons are constantly reinforced by all teachers throughout the day, seems to be the most effective method. Other options include teaching formal character lessons in a particular subject, with the responsibility rotated weekly among subject areas, or teaching the lessons in homeroom or at another designated time during the school day. A few pros and cons of these methods are shown in the table on page 58. Some schools may choose to implement a pre-set program, in which lessons and materials are provided by the company supplying the program. A number of good programs are available, particularly for elementary grades. Regardless of the approach you choose, realize that character education is most successful when it is emphasized throughout the entire school.

Saturation teaching

With this method, students are "saturated" with character-related teaching. The traits are modeled, taught, and reinforced throughout the day by all school staff. Through repeated emphasis, students are reminded continually of the character traits and cannot miss the message. More than any other approach, saturation teaching requires buy-in from the entire staff. The participation of all teachers is needed, and auxiliary staff such as bus drivers, secretaries, custodians, and security guards are an important part of such programs. This method requires more work and coordination than other methods, however, and some staff members may view it as "too much, too fast," particularly if the idea of character education is new. Saturation teaching also takes a longer period of time to implement fully.

Single-class instruction

With this method, character traits are assigned to particular departments, and teachers in that department are expected to develop and teach short daily lessons on the trait. Instruction is typically rotated among departments weekly or monthly. Other teachers may choose to emphasize the weekly trait as well, but they aren't expected to do so in a formal way. This method has worked very well in middle schools. If your school takes this approach, be sure that all teachers refer to and otherwise show their support for the character traits that are being taught.

Daily instruction at a specific time

For younger students, it's very effective to teach character lessons during homeroom or at a specific time of the day and then to rein-

There are as many "right" ways to teach character as there are schools.

Pros and Cons of Character Education Approaches

Method	Pros	Cons
Saturation teaching	• Fastest way to success when done effectively • Students can't miss the message • Involvement of all staff helps transform the entire school culture	• Requires continuous attention to character education by all staff members; some may be unwilling to commit to it • Time- and labor-intensive
Single-class instruction	• Relatively easy to coordinate • Responsibility is shared among teachers • Does not require daily attention from all teachers	• No way to ensure that all staff are teaching the character traits • Some students may be missed
Daily instruction at a specific time	• Lends itself to uniform lessons • Predictability	• Can become just another "subject"

force those lessons throughout the day. Although this method works well in elementary schools, it isn't as effective among high school students.

Other methods

Finally, some schools use a particular department to teach the character lessons, such as the Social Studies or English departments. While this approach may raise awareness of character traits among students, it will not have the same tranformative effect on the school environment as a more thorough method.

Deciding on the Character Traits

It can seem like an overwhelming task to decide which character traits you will teach in a given year. After all, there are many traits that deserve attention. Even though you could probably come up with a long list of worthy traits, most schools teach essentially the same traits, with some variations among synonyms and from year to year. A good way to begin developing a list of traits for your school is to brainstorm around the question: "What qualities do we want to see in our students?" By identifying the character traits most needed at your school, you have already started customizing the character education program to your unique school community. Effective character education can never be a "one size fits all" initiative.

After the committee has developed a list of character traits to consider, evaluate the list to see if any traits could be easily combined, such as "polite" and "good manners." Use multi-voting to choose the traits which

> Effective character education can never be a "one size fits all" initiative.

are most important for your school this year. For example, let's say your committee has decided to teach 18 different traits during the school year (a different trait every two weeks). On a large flip chart (or several sheets of flip chart paper), list all of the traits you've come up with during brainstorming. Give each committee member 12 "votes" (best represented by colorful stick-on dots), and have them put one sticker beside each of their top 12 traits. By looking at which traits received the most stickers, it will quickly become apparent which 18 traits are favored.

Once you have determined which traits are most important to you as a committee, give other staff members and perhaps selected students an opportunity to voice their opinions. Type up the list of 18 traits and send it to the entire staff, asking each staff member to rank their top 12 traits. Do the same with a group of student leaders and with your parent association, if you have one. By combining the results from staff, students, and parents, you'll get an overall view of which character traits are most important to the stakeholders in your school. Place particular emphasis on these traits during the first year of your character program.

In subsequent years, repeat the process by asking, "What character traits do we want our students to exhibit?" Many issues will move to the forefront during the first year of the character program. To keep the program fresh, the committee will want to change the sequence in which character traits are taught, add and/or delete certain traits, and rotate who is teaching what. You'll also want to find new materials, delete what hasn't worked well, and develop new programs. Keep the program changing so that students—and staff—don't get tired of character education.

Encouraging Staff Buy-In

When you start asking other teachers to incorporate character lessons into their classrooms, you are asking them to support the program. Getting this buy-in is not always easy—in fact, it can prove to be downright challenging. A few considerations can help tremendously on this front: First and foremost, keep the staff members informed of what you are doing. Second, give them an opportunity to have a voice in the process. Third, be considerate of their needs.

- **Keep staff members informed.** Without overdoing it, share memos and news articles with the entire staff so that they know what is going on throughout the country regarding character education. Make sure that all staff members understand how the character traits will be taught and what will be expected of them. Host at least one annual character education forum; use this forum as a chance to talk as well as to listen—they may have some great ideas. Invite your business sponsors to attend and to underwrite the forum; their presence and support will lend weight to the program. If at all possible, pay the staff members to attend. (Even if some people only come for the extra hour of pay, they will hear the message nonetheless and go away with a better knowledge of character education.)

- **Give them a chance to participate.** No one likes to feel that they have no choice in a particular matter. Look for ways to give staff members a voice in making major decisions, such as which traits will be taught at your school in the coming year.

Common traits used in character education programs

It may be useful for your committee to see a list of traits that are frequently emphasized in other character programs. Use the list below as a guideline for generating your own ideas about which character traits should be emphasized at your school.

Responsible	Fairness
Compassionate	Self-Control
Kind	Citizenship
Punctual	Generous
Reliable	Respectful
Cheerful	Economical
Positive Attitude	Optimistic
Empathetic	Initiative
Perseverance	Joyful
Patient	Ambitious
Good Sport	Tolerant
Courageous	Gracious
Honest	Considerate
Trustworthy	Creative
Resourceful	Caring
Self-Respect	Loyal
Polite	Thankful
Dependable	Cooperative

Issues that can weaken your program

Certain attitudes and behaviors can seriously undermine your character program. We can identify at least seven problems that will keep your school from being transformed by its character program:

- Lack of support from the administration

- Poor planning

- Lack of follow-through

- Lack of modeling by school staff

- Lack of enthusiasm

- Committee meetings that drag on and on

- Expectation of immediate change

Do what you can to make sure your program isn't derailed by one of these issues.

For example, you could give all the staff members 10 votes each and let them "multi-vote" for the 10 character traits they feel are most important for your school (chosen from a list prepared by the committee). With this input, committee members can then make final decisions about which traits will be emphasized.

- **Be considerate.** If you are expecting teachers to incorporate character-related lessons, be sure that they have resources at their disposal for developing those lessons. Keep them informed of special assemblies, and vary the time of day that assemblies are held so you do not intrude too often on a single person's classroom time. Serve refreshments at special staff events—and particularly when they are a captive audience.

The importance of support staff

Remember to include the school's support staff in your character education program. Every person who interacts with students throughout the day contributes to how students view the "character" of their school. At a minimum, provide an in-service for auxiliary staff members to inform them of the program, and share regular updates with them about the program's successes. These staff members have numerous opportunities to reinforce character traits with students.

- Persons who handle discipline, such as assistant principals and counselors, have frequent opportunities to help students distinguish what is right and what is expected in specific (and often difficult) situations.

> Support staff can add dimension to your program by reinforcing good character outside of the classrooms.

- Secretaries and office staff are very visible liaisons with parents and the community. How they handle persons on the phone or visitors to the school speaks volumes about the atmosphere at the school.

- Bus drivers are the first people to see students in the morning and the last ones to see them after school. Bus drivers can set the tone for the school day by expecting students to exhibit good character from the very beginning.

- Custodians are in the building all day and are often in contact with students in the halls. Mutual respect should be the norm.

- Cafeteria workers also interact with students daily as students go through the lunch lines. Meal time is another opportunity to reinforce good character.

- If your school has security guards, how those guards deal with students can add to or detract from the overall school emphasis on character.

(**Note:** You'll want to be careful about what you expect these staff members to do in support of the character education program. In some areas, employees have strict job descriptions which must be respected.)

Dealing with naysayers

In virtually every school, a few persons will refuse to participate in the school's emphasis on character education; some even may be openly

Success Tip: Whenever you get staff (or parents) together to talk about the character education program, *feed them*. Providing refreshments is a personal touch that helps make the atmosphere more informal. Some homemade cookies and a pot of coffee go a long way toward generating good will and breaking down barriers between people.

hostile. In this situation, school administrators have a responsibility to stress the importance of teamwork, but even they may not be effective. If you have naysayers in your school—people who are strongly opposed and vocal about it—be kind to them and keep trying to gain their support. Listen to their objections and try to understand where they are coming from, if you can, but don't feel that you have to constantly defend the program. As time goes on, many of these people will be won over as they see changes in the school environment, improvements in student attitudes, and fewer discipline problems in their classrooms. Students will still benefit a great deal from the teachings of those committed to the program. Keep your eyes on the goal!

Making Your Message Consistent

As you think of how you will teach character to your students, consider that the informal messages you send to students are equally as important as formal lessons. Does your school environment demonstrate respect for students? How can you make changes that let students know you respect them and are counting on them to be respectful in return? Take the school cafeteria, for example. What can be done to improve the eating environment in your school cafeteria? Some schools have used laminated placemats with character traits printed on them as a way to reinforce the traits and to encourage an atmosphere of caring about the mealtime environment. As you move forward with your character education program, you'll want to examine these subtle messages and make improvements as needed.

There are many ways to incorporate character education into your school's curriculum. The most effective program is one that is tailored to meet the needs of your unique population of students.

Chapter 5

Developing Student Advocates

"If children don't have an outlet—a chance to be heard—they will keep their voices inside along with their gifts."
—Sobonfu E. Somé, <u>Welcoming Spirit Home</u>

Today's students are looking for positive ways to be involved in their communities. A character education program can provide meaningful and satisfying avenues for such involvement. Getting students involved in the character program as soon as possible is to your advantage. By helping students develop into advocates—kids who support and promote good character among their peers—the program will reap long-term benefits for the students, their families, and the school. As the character program grows, there will be many opportunities to mentor individual students in developing their leadership skills. With the help of student leaders, the entire school can become more keenly aware of the importance of good character.

Students are the very best proponents of good character that you can have in your school because they use peer pressure in ways that adults cannot. Most students will gladly remind each other of the character traits when they see problems. There are many avenues for getting students involved in the program, and the students often have great ideas on how they can help promote good character at their school. What they need from the character committee is leadership, encouragement, and help with organization.

Keep in mind that the students who become leaders in your character program may not be the same students who are leaders in other clubs. In fact, it's a good idea to look outside of existing school groups to

Advocates

Students who support and promote good character among their peers

Get students involved in activities that put good character into action.

identify students with untapped leadership potential. By observing students in the halls, classrooms, cafeteria, and at after-school functions, you will probably be able to identify student leaders who are just waiting to be "discovered." As teachers, we must always remember that kids need encouragement to figure out what their abilities and talents are. Providing opportunities to be involved in a positive group can open doors for many students.

Opportunities for student involvement are endless. Student-related activities can be roughly divided into on-going programs and special events. Try to have a mix of both types of activities to keep students involved and interested in the program.

On-Going Programs

Character clubs

A character-related student club is a good way to promote character and service in the school and community. This club can take many different forms, depending on the needs and culture of your particular school. Use the ideas below as a starting point for potential activities, then challenge your students to develop their own projects.

- Initiate school-wide projects such as "Campus Clean-Up Day" or "Dress For Success Day."

- Organize a holiday toy or food drive, then have students assist in delivering the toys or food to the distributing agency (or to the recipients themselves, in some cases).

Success Tip: As students gain experience in the program, slowly let them assume greater leadership roles in the student group. Encourage older students to lead the younger students. As much as possible, encourage your students to make this "their" group.

- Develop activities that can be shared with other schools, such as a reading club, a puppet show, or another entertainment group related to the theme of good character.

- Volunteer at a senior center, a homeless shelter, a child care center, or a Meals on Wheels program, to mention a few.

- Participate in a fundraiser for a local hospital or charitable organization.

- Organize a neighborhood clean-up campaign.

- Set up a recycling program in the school.

- Use the Internet to get involved in a social project with students in another country.

Students in specialized groups can give powerful testimonials for the program. You may want to form a character-related speech team—a group of students who are willing to give speeches about the character program outside of the school. Using student speakers is very effective with adults and with other students, provided the speeches are appropriate for the audience. Another excellent way to involve students in the character program is to form a music or dance team that focuses on character-related issues. Be sure that someone on the committee is willing to work with the group (or groups) regularly to help the students develop and practice their speeches, songs, or dance routines.

Choosing students for character-related groups is a delicate process. You want the club to be open to all students, yet you want to emphasize that students involved in the group must be willing to support and promote good character. One way to screen students is to use an application for membership that requires the students to write about why they want to be involved in the club. If you use applications, this is a good time to obtain parental permission for the child's involvement: simply print the permission statement at the bottom of the application and require that it be signed before the student may participate. Careful reading of the applications can help you identify students with undiscovered leadership potential.

Student assemblies

Student assemblies can be used in various ways to promote the character program, depending on the ages of your students. Weekly or monthly assemblies work well with elementary students, particularly when the children themselves are performing skits or sharing stories about the character traits. Assemblies are more effective with children through 8th grade; for high school students, focused presentations by professional groups typically have a greater impact. If your program is well-funded, you may be able to take advantage of professional groups that perform character-related programs. For middle-school students, you may want to have a character-related assembly once each semester or grading period. As much as possible, involve your students in planning the assemblies. Alternately, you may choose to add a character-related message to existing assemblies.

Be sure to get parental permission

It is very important to have parental permission for students to be involved in any activity that may result in them being photographed or videotaped. The permission slip signed by parents should state that the parent gives his/her permission for the child to be involved in the program and for the child's likeness and/or words to be used to promote the program. Make this permission a prerequisite for student involvement.

Awards and recognition

You may want to present character-based awards to students at regular assemblies. Types of awards could include:

- Poster and essay contest winners

- Student of character (selected monthly, quarterly, or yearly; for students who consistently demonstrate good character)

- Student of promise (selected as appropriate; for students who show promise in their character development)

- Most improved behavior (awarded at the end of the school year to students who have made significant changes in their behavior at school)

- Scholarship winners (awarded to students who exhibit outstanding character in their daily lives)

It isn't necessary to spend a lot of money on these awards. Students are often encouraged and pleased with an attractive certificate and a praising letter to his or her parents, written on school stationery. You could also mention award winners over the public address system during school-wide announcements, ask teachers to recognize the students in class, or have the school principal deliver awards to students in class. Display pictures of the award winners in a showcase or in the hallway or cafeteria; students love to see pictures of themselves and their peers.

Television

In-school television can be very helpful in spreading character messages school-wide. Furthermore, it allows you to provide short character-related programs without changing students' daily routines. Enlist the help of different classes, departments, student organizations, choirs, and drama groups to perform the televised messages. A group of students could act out a character trait, perform skits, sing character-related songs, or read definitions of particular traits. Students are likely to hear more of the message and to think about it longer when it comes from their peers.

Another way to use classroom television effectively is to show a selected character-related video to all classes at a specific time and provide teachers with follow-up questions for discussing the program. The week before a school vacation is usually a good time to schedule this type of event. To be effective, it's important that the teachers are willing to discuss and reinforce concepts presented in the video. To this end, it may be helpful to allow teachers to preview the video before it is shown to students.

Special Events

Special events can be used to build excitement around the character program and keep it from becoming stale. They are also a good way to involve civic and corporate sponsors, who are usually willing to provide speakers or other personnel for the event.

Leadership Challenge Day

A "Leadership Challenge Day" can be very effective in helping students develop as leaders. With this event, a group of students is chosen to spend a day devoted to the subject of leadership. You'll want to involve students from every activity and/or every classroom. Structure the day with a combination of discussions, activities, and a keynote talk by an inspirational speaker. Ask your guest speaker to challenge the students to be leaders in their school, their community, and the world. If possible, conduct the event at an off-school location. (One of your corporate sponsors might have a conference room you could use, for example.) During the course of the day, find out what the students want to be involved in, what kinds of programs they think will be effective with their peers, and what they see as problems within the school. Share stories of students who have made a difference in other schools. Brainstorm with them, then make plans to implement at least one of their ideas in the near future. End the day with a small service project.

Business Forum

A "Business Forum" is an excellent way to help students understand how character is relevant to the workplace. Invite business leaders to give short classroom presentations on the importance of good character in their jobs or places of employment, and allow time for questions. To reach as many students as possible, arrange to have 10-20 speakers presenting in different "host" classrooms. Assign students from the character club (if you have one) to escort each guest speaker around the building. Such a forum will be particularly interesting to high school students, who are anxious to work and to be success-

Working with other school organizations

As your character program becomes more active, you may find that your committee's plans are constantly bumping into or conflicting with the plans of other school organizations. To avoid problems with other groups, try to get your activities listed on the school calendar as early as possible. You may have to follow up diligently, particularly at a large school where many events are vying for time. You will need to work closely with the school activity director.

Co-sponsor as many special events as you can with other student groups. Working together in this way will benefit your program and will reinforce the concept that good character is integral at your school. Plan to work closely with the other school club chairpersons. If someone else steps on what you see as your "turf," look for opportunities to co-sponsor the event in question rather than be offended. The more students that are involved in the character program, the greater likelihood of success at creating positive change in your school. Greet each problem with the expectation that you can find a solution, and when you cannot find a solution, be willing to change. A positive attitude and the desire to collaborate with other groups will help the character program be better accepted by students and staff members alike.

ful at their jobs. The forum also provides a golden opportunity for students to meet employers and for employers to meet potential employees. A well-organized Business Forum can serve as a catalyst for involving the surrounding community at your school.

Scholarships

As your program grows, you may want to approach local businesses or community organizations to sponsor a character scholarship program. (In fact, you may find that the businesses approach you!) Scholarships can be awarded to a graduating senior (or seniors, depending on your scholarship fund) who has consistently represented good character both in the school and in the community. You could also provide scholarships for students to attend summer leadership camps or other local summer programs. Try to keep these scholarships separate from grades (above a minimum standard, of course), as a student with average grades may consistently exhibit better character than a student with top grades. It's helpful for the committee to decide the criteria for receiving the awards well in advance of giving them out. This helps make the selection process more objective.

Using Incentives

The use of incentives as part of a character program is controversial. Many schools use incentives to encourage the development of good habits in students—a practice that is similar to parents using gold stars or giving additional allowance when children do their chores. In effect, using incentives says to students, "Your conduct at school is so important that we will reward you when we see it improving or when we see you developing the habits that are necessary for our school to have a good environment." The tangible rewards help students develop habits. Good habits, once in place, continue to remind the students of good character throughout life.

Some educators oppose using incentives to reward students for good character, though, because they maintain that the "feeling" resulting from good character is reward enough. Others feel that this may be a reasonable argument for adults, but children are motivated differently. Children need constant and meaningful feedback, particularly when developing new habits. Rewards provide that feedback. To earn incentives, students must both internalize the message and demonstrate it in their environment. Just as grades are used (however imperfectly) to measure mastery of a subject, incentives provide a measure of how well students are mastering the concept of good character.

Incentives are particularly useful for children in the younger and middle grades. At these ages, children are very motivated by recognition and by what they can "show" for their efforts. Incentives are less useful in upper grades; older teens are more likely to be motivated by a sense of "rightness." This developing idea of what is "right" is a good reflection of the students' increasing maturity.

One incentive program uses "character coupons" that the students can exchange for items donated by local businesses, such as pens, T-shirts, and other small items. Every staff member receives a certain number of coupons each month to give to students. Because the coupons are valuable and limited, the staff use them discriminately to reward students who

Success Tip: It's a very good idea to help other school groups with their projects in exchange for help with yours. Over time this kind of collaboration can lead to a school-wide focus that includes character education in every activity and organization.

truly deserve recognition. An incentive program can always be abused, of course, but the advantages usually far outweigh the disadvantages.

If you choose to use incentives in your character education program, plan and manage that reward system carefully. Take care to avoid the pitfall of "entitlement," wherein students start expecting rewards for basic behaviors such as coming to school or not being late for class. To be effective, the incentives should be used for true demonstrations of good character rather than for just showing up or for not being disruptive.

Mentoring Student Advocates

As you identify a core group of students who are willing to promote good character in your school, look for opportunities to involve them in the larger movement. You will find numerous ways to mentor these students as your program develops. A few ideas include:

- When you are asked to speak to a community or business group, take a few students with you. Include the students in your presentation by letting each one speak for 3 minutes (or less) on how the program has affected them. Be sure to help them with their speeches beforehand and give them a chance to practice.

- Organize a student exchange with another nearby school where students are making a difference. Ask each of your participating students to identify one practice from the other school that could be incorporated into your school's program. Have them present these ideas to the character committee.

- Set up a joint meeting between a group of student leaders and the character committee. Do this at least once a year, preferably once each semester. In the meeting, brainstorm together on ways to encourage student involvement, and solicit students' feedback on ways to improve the program. The joint meeting provides a valuable "reality check" for the committee and gives students a voice in the program.

- If possible, invite a student advocate to accompany you when you give a school tour to visitors who are interested in the character program. Solicit input from the student as you are pointing out various aspects of your program to the guests. Also, arrange time for a group of students to answer questions from the visitors about their views of the character program. Try to keep the setting informal, and serve a snack if possible.

- Once each year, give students in the character club an evaluation form asking them for feedback on what the program has meant to them. Also ask how they would change or improve the club. This written evaluation provides you with comments in the students' own words that you can use when promoting the program to staff members and outside of the school.

- Reward your student group with extras from time to time—little things such as pizza, tickets to games, or other small prizes. Be sure to thank them constantly.

The success of a character education program is seen most clearly in the lives of the students and in the climate of the school.

Chapter 6

Cultivating Parent Support

"A school system without parents at its foundation is just like a bucket with a hole in it."
—*Rev. Jesse L. Jackson*

Character education begins in the home, and a school-based character program is actually an extension of that home training. In many families the school program will reinforce concepts parents are already teaching. In other families, where parents are not available or are unable to teach good character, the school program can provide guidance that would otherwise be lacking in students' lives. When talking with parents, always emphasize that the school is reinforcing concepts they are teaching at home. Communication is key here: make sure that parents know what character traits you are teaching so there is a strong link between home and school.

It's wise to involve parents in the character program from the very beginning. Some schools routinely include parents on the character committee, while other schools do not. Either way, parents should always be welcome to attend a meeting and express their ideas or concerns. At the beginning of each school year, hold a forum where parents can come and learn about the program. The subject of "character" can be touchy among some parents, but knowing what is happening at school is usually enough to allay their parental concerns. After all, very few parents are going to object to an added emphasis on respect, responsibility, self-control, or kindness!

Methods for Involving Parents

There are many different ways to involve parents in the character program. Committee members should constantly be looking for new

Whenever possible, provide parents with information about the school's character program and ways that they can be involved.

ways to enlist the support of parents. Ideally, the program will be most successful if teachers are echoing at school the lessons being taught at home. In reality, though, for some children it may be the teachers who are providing the primary character instruction.

You can't do too much to involve parents! Use every tool available and use it often. Listed below are some ideas for getting parents on board.

- Sponsor a character education forum for parents at least once per year, with a guest speaker or speakers, an overview of the school's character program, and time for questions. Choose speakers who are entertaining but who also can address the needs of parents and students. Schedule two different sessions to accommodate parents' work schedules: one in the afternoon and another in the evening. Serve refreshments.

- Publicize the character program at the school Open House (or Parents' Night) and during parent-teacher conferences. To do this, set up a booth or table in a prominent location and provide printed materials on character education. Include information or a display board about your school's program, along with copies of relevant newspaper articles and information on character-related resources. If possible, have a committee member available to answer parents' questions.

- Be sure that every parent newsletter contains a message about character education. Call it a "Character Corner" or some

Success Tip: Recognize that many parents don't know *how* to instill good character in their children. Make it a priority to provide resources that will help them teach good character.

other catchy phrase. Try to keep it in the same spot on the page from one newsletter to the next so parents can find it easily.

- Encourage parents to be involved in special character-related events. Interested parents can be a great source of volunteer help for these events and for character projects.

- Invite parents to all character-related programs. Make a point of calling parents whose children are performing in a program, and personally invite them to attend.

- Have a member of the character committee speak at a PTA or parent meeting at least once each year. Provide an overview of the program, including some of the positive comments you've heard from students and staff. For added impact, recruit several students to speak about good character at the meeting.

- Develop a calendar which lists the character traits that will be taught each week. Send a copy of the calendar home with every student at the beginning of the school year. Using the calendar, parents will know what traits you are teaching each week and can reinforce those traits at home. If your school district is already providing calendars or agendas for students and/or parents, be sure the character traits and definitions are listed there. You can also use the calendar to provide parents with ideas for helping their children think about character issues.

- In elementary schools, use weekly flyers to continually remind parents about the school's character initiative and to give them tips for reinforcing the concepts.

Handling Parent Objections

It is rare that parents will object to character education in the school. When they do, their objections usually fall into one of two categories:

1. Antagonism because they feel you are taking over their job or telling them they are not doing it well, or
2. Concern that you are teaching your "values" to their children.

If you encounter a parent who is strongly opposed to the program, a good first step is to invite that parent to meet with you and the principal or with the character committee. (Don't offer to meet with the parent alone—two of you will be better at countering objections than one.) Explain the reasons why the school or district has decided to include a character program, and provide details on how the program will operate. Give the parent as much printed literature on the subject as you can find; this will help him or her understand the size of the character movement and how it is transforming schools. Encourage the parent to express what it is he or she is objecting to—specifically, which character trait do they not want taught to their child? Usually you will find that the parent doesn't really object to the traits, but has some misunderstandings about the program itself. Try to explain the intent of the program and thereby counter the objections. Then, invite the parent to become involved in the program and be a force for positive change in the school.

Parents have more influence on the character of their children than anyone else. Enlisting their support will magnify the impact of the school's program.

Chapter 7

Involving the Community

> *"Developing one's character is a social act. We exist and are raised within a social milieu—within a web of human connections."*
> —*Kevin Ryan & Karen Bohlin, <u>Building Character in Schools</u>*

Your local community can be a pillar of support for the character program. Civic organizations and businesses can provide both tangible and intangible support. Churches can reinforce character traits in their programs, and the local news media can be instrumental in building awareness and excitement around the program. As a committee, you'll want to take a close look at the resources in your community and engage them in support of the program. Make it a goal to involve as many different community groups as you can.

Community Organizations

There are many community organizations who could be good partners for your school's character program, and these organizations are usually keenly interested in helping students develop into good citizens. Call the leaders of these groups and talk with them about the character program. You may be pleasantly surprised to discover that you and they have similar goals, and that opportunities for collaboration are endless.

Rotary International

Local chapters of Rotary International are very active in many cities, providing tangible support for schools and school programs. Rotary is a volunteer organization of business and civic leaders whose aim is to provide humanitarian service, encourage high ethical standards in all vocations, and help build goodwill and peace.

Character education is very consistent with their mission, and Rotary Clubs have been instrumental in underwriting and supporting character education in a number of U.S. communities.

Kiwanis International

Kiwanis is a volunteer organization that seeks to promote service and international goodwill; it focuses predominantly on programs that affect children. In addition to many adult chapters, Kiwanis International also sponsors service clubs for young people on college campuses and in high schools and middle schools. Local Kiwanis clubs sponsor thousands of service projects each year.

Churches and religious groups

Local churches and religious groups can be a tremendous asset in reinforcing the character program. You may want to approach these groups and let them know what you are doing in the school. Point out that they can help by emphasizing the importance of good character in their programs. If there is a ministerial association in your area, give them a copy of your character education plan. They may want to help by promoting the specific character traits in their lessons, children's sermons, and after-school programs. It certainly doesn't hurt the character program to keep these groups informed of your efforts, and it may be very beneficial.

If religious organizations are a strong social force in your community, try to keep them "in the loop." In one city where character education was implemented in all the schools, the school district provided religious leaders with an entire notebook on the pro-

Success Tip: In some communities, clergy members have strongly opposed a school's character program, claiming that the school is taking over the function of the church. If this happens in your area, invite the opponents to become members of the character committee, and welcome their input. This will give them a voice in the initiative and help defuse the idea that the school is in competition with the church. Even if an opponent declines to be involved with the committee, keep him or her informed about what you are doing in the school; be sure to highlight the successes of the program as they occur.

gram. This district also publishes a monthly newsletter on the program to help keep church groups informed.

Neighborhood associations

Some communities have active neighborhood associations that might be willing to support the program; communities which border the school property are likely to be particularly interested. Call persons from these associations and see if there are opportunities to collaborate on neighborhood clean-ups or other projects. For example, you may find that school neighbors are willing to put signs in their yards during special initiatives. Make friends with your school's neighbors.

Local charitable groups

Nearly every community has non-profit groups, such as hospital or university foundations, that are working to create positive changes in the area. When these groups come to your attention, look for potential ways to collaborate.

Local government and utilities

When thinking of ways to involve the community in your school's character program, don't forget about the local government and businesses such as utilities. These organizations can support the program in many ways.

News Media

The news media can greatly enhance your school's visibility in the community—for good or for bad. Often it is the negative stories that make

Businesses can play a key role in supporting character education in their communities.

it into the news; you may find that it takes a lot of effort and political pull to get newspapers and TV news programs to focus on positive things happening in the schools. Make it a point to keep trying. Call your local news media—newspapers, TV stations, and radio stations—and find out which reporters are in charge of community reporting. Get to know those people by inviting them to speak to your students on local issues. Encourage students to write letters to them, sharing positive things that are happening at the school. Keep your media contacts informed of newsworthy events, such as business/school collaborations and special community projects.

One caution: Don't assume that news coverage of the character program will be positive. When giving interviews to reporters, choose your words carefully. The issues of character, ethics, and values are often confused and can be quite inflammatory.

Businesses

The students of today are the employees of tomorrow. For this reason, businesses are typically very supportive of character education programs in the schools—they know that character education helps students develop the skills they will need to become good employees. Time and money used to help students learn basic skills, such as punctuality, responsibility, and self-control, are seen as good investments in the future work force.

To identify potential corporate sponsors for your program, use the following categories to list businesses that committee members could contact:

- Companies already sponsoring school programs
- Merchants located near the school grounds or ones popular with students
- Larger employers in the area
- Businesses where you have an "in"
- Local cooperative business alliances

Before approaching individual businesses for their support, decide as a committee what you want from them. As much as possible, look for non-monetary ways to involve businesses; they will be more likely to support the program if they can do so in ways other than giving cash. Be creative here—there are many ways that companies can support your program. Some suggestions include:

- Posting character-related signs on the business marquis.
- Offering discount coupons for use in the incentive program.
- Providing products or services for use in the incentive program.
- Donating use of their conference facilities for occasional off-site events.
- Sending employees to speak on the importance of character at a special school event.
- Participating in the school's "Career Day" or "Business Forum."
- Donating the printing of materials such as a character calendar or parent newsletter.
- Becoming a corporate sponsor of your school.
- Participating in exchange programs with teachers, so teachers can experience the business environment and business employees can experience the school environment.

- Loaning an employee to help with a specialized issue. For example, a non-profit organization may have a staff expert in fundraising who could advise the committee; a manufacturing organization might have a trained facilitator who could act as facilitator for the character committee.

As the program becomes established and its successes become known, you may find that area companies will see the results and want to be involved with your character program. In fact, business leaders may approach you with ideas on how they can be involved.

Giving Back to the Community

Finally, even as you hope to find support and resources for the character program from your local community, remember that giving is a two-way street. Whenever possible, get students involved in projects that benefit the community. This will raise student awareness of local needs and, hopefully, help them mature into adults who are more willing to be involved in their communities.

Whenever possible, get students involved in projects that benefit their community.

Chapter 8

Building Excitement at Your School

"Nothing is so contagious as enthusiasm; it moves stones, it charms brutes. Enthusiasm is the genius of sincerity, and trust accomplishes no victories without it."
—*Edward Bulwer-Lytton*

Any character program will be more successful if it is fun and exciting. Constantly be on the lookout for ways to build excitement at your school. Beginning the year with a grand kick-off event is a great way to announce the character program to new students and to remind continuing students that good character is important at their school. By varying the media you use, you can saturate the environment with your message without seeming redundant. Students and staff will quickly become bored if the same approach is used over and over again. Keep finding new ways to call attention to good character.

Start with a Kick-Off

Begin the character program each year with a grand kick-off. Make it a day of excitement and surprises. You want students to feel like this is going to be something fun, not something moralistic or "preachy." A few suggestions:

- Hire an entertaining guest speaker or musical artist to address students at an assembly.

- Use the in-school public address system to reinforce the program with students and staff. Skits or plays written by and starring students will attract a lot of attention.

- Award prizes randomly throughout the day.

- Have someone dressed as the school mascot roaming the halls. Decorate the mascot with buttons of all the character traits that you will teach during the year.

- Sponsor character-related contests in the classrooms. (Make these up!)

- Send a letter home to parents detailing how character traits will be taught throughout the year.

Vary Your Media

When coming up with ways to build excitement around the character program, leave no stone unturned. Use every outlet available to you so that kids are saturated with the message. Just as a steady stream of water can wear down the largest rock, so too steady efforts to incorporate character into your curriculum will slowly change the learning environment at your school. (That in itself will be exciting!) As much as possible, vary the media you use to present the character message.

Be seen everywhere

Visual reminders help students absorb the message of good character. Make sure that "character" is everywhere they look. Use banners at entrances to herald the character program, and put flyers, signs, or posters throughout the building. Change these often—as much as every week if your program highlights a different trait each week. Keep the visual stimuli shifting so that you continue to catch students' attention. If your school has glass showcases, claim one for the character program; you can use it to display prizes, to post students' pictures, or for various initiatives sponsored by the student character group. Engage students in a poster contest, for example, then display the winning posters prominently.

Write about it

Printed materials are very helpful in reaching parents with the idea of good character. If your school sends a weekly bulletin to parents, use it to give them ideas for reinforcing the character traits at home. Send letters to parents outlining the program and what traits you will be teaching throughout the year. Whenever you have successes to report, be sure that parents hear about them. If your students have school agendas, send notes home to parents via the agendas. At least once each year, involve students in an essay contest around the theme of good character. Publicize the winners of the contest and, if possible, read the winning essays in every class or over the public address (PA) system.

Use audiovisual to your advantage

Using your PA system and Channel 1 (the in-school video system present in many schools), you can reach all students simultaneously with the same message. Today's kids are accustomed to multimedia, so use it often. Have the school principal announce the character trait being focused on each week by reading the definition over the PA system. Broadcast catchy character-related songs. Show short movie clips and videos school-wide. If possible, include skits and videos prepared by students.

Keep the special events coming

Special events throughout the year help keep people interested in the program. In this category, the possibilities are truly endless. You can have events for parents, for teachers and staff, and for students. Initiatives and events help remind everyone that your school is committed to developing good character in students.

By planning ahead, you can keep the program evolving and changing. Be on the lookout for ideas that can be adapted and used in the program. A dynamic program does much to keep the enthusiasm and interest of staff and students.

Encourage a Shared Vision

Your school's character education program will be most effective if committee members (and teachers) have a shared vision for what the program can accomplish. It may take some time to develop such a vision, but positive changes in the school environment will help build excitement and a sense of possibility among the committee members. Generally speaking, the people who are attracted to the committee are those who already have a sense of what character education can accomplish. It then becomes a matter of cultivating that vision throughout your particular school.

Some ideas for cultivating vision:

- Relate another school's experience. There are many success stories of schools that have been transformed as a result of character education. Find short articles about such schools,

> With shared vision and a team approach, committee members will find themselves excited by the idea of "flying" with the program.

and make it a practice to read one of these "vision articles" aloud at the beginning or end of each meeting.

- Have a "what if" session. Using a large flip chart or chalkboard to record the answers, ask committee members to complete the statement "What if ..." For example, "What if ... none of our students swore in the halls?" or "What if ... parents thanked us for teaching their children?" This is an informal way to help cultivate a sense of possibility among the committee. Keep the session relaxed by serving refreshments, but set a definite time limit (20 minutes, perhaps). Ask someone to type up the statements and distribute them at the next meeting. Periodically you can revisit this list, particularly if someone has a success to report.

- Find some new ideas. Purchase copies of the book *Educating for Character*, by Thomas Lickona, for each committee member. This is a great "idea book" and is pertinent to every type of character education program. Ask each member to read a different chapter and report back to the committee on the key points in that chapter.

- Attend a character education conference. Conferences are a great place to get "the big picture" on character education. It's exciting to meet people from all over the country (or all over the world) who are committed to the same task. Many useful ideas can be gathered from the experiences of other teachers and other schools. If funds are not available for travel to national conferences, consider attending state-wide or local conferences. (See the Resource Guide for a list of character-related organizations, many of whom sponsor conferences.)

To help committee members remain enthusiastic about the program, keep the information flowing. Pass out copies of pertinent articles at every meeting so the committee members will know what is going on in the field of character education. Most of your committee members will not take the time to look for this information themselves or to go to conferences on the topic. It becomes your task, then, to help them develop a bigger picture than just what's occurring at your school. If a committee member brings you an article related to character education, ask him or her to share the article with the group at the next meeting.

Be sure to provide positive reinforcement as well. Always keep your eyes open for opportunities to thank your committee members. Leave thank-you notes in their office mailboxes or in their classrooms. Make a point to thank them in committee meetings also. If someone has handled a particularly difficult event or situation well, compliment that person. We all like to know that our efforts are noticed and appreciated by others.

Whenever possible, find reasons to celebrate even the smallest of victories. Try to share with the committee any and all positive comments you hear from students and parents. Use any excuse to bring in food to the meetings; people love to snack. When you reach a milestone, such as half-way through the year, give goofy prizes to each of your committee members. Make it fun.

Seeking recognition for your school is another way to help committee members stay enthusiastic. Many of our schools are maligned in their communities because of high-profile problems such as drug use and violence. Find ways to publicize the good things happening at your school through the local news media and community organizations. As the word gets out that things are changing at your school, committee members and other staff members will take more interest in the program and greater pride in being a part of that change.

Include teachers and staff

As you are thinking about how to build excitement in the school, don't forget about creating excitement for teachers and staff as well. For the character program to be a success, you really need their help. As much as possible, make it easy for them—it's hard for anyone to get excited when all the hoopla is seen as "more work for me to do." Teachers need resources for ideas on how to incorporate character into their subjects— they will appreciate it if the committee leaves a new set of ideas in their mailboxes with each new character trait. For the sake of courtesy, explain initiatives and special programs to teachers well in advance of letting the information become known to students.

Similarly, non-teaching staff members should be kept informed about upcoming programs and how they can help. Administrative staff often play key roles as liaisons with parents and are more likely to work one-on-one with students. Support staff such as security guards, cafeteria workers, and maintenance personnel have many opportunities to interact with students and to reinforce the program. They should feel empowered to do so.

Be Aware of Burn-Out

Finally, don't forget to take care of yourself. You'll be spending a lot of energy trying to get students, parents, and teachers excited about character education. In the process you may find yourself getting very tired, even burned out. When this happens, do something proactive that helps rebuild your enthusiasm. You might be recharged by sharing your results with other schools, or by crunching some numbers to see just how effective the program has been (comparing attendance, discipline referrals, or other objective criteria, for example). You might enjoy attending a regional or national conference to interact with other teachers who are implementing character programs at their schools. Conferences are a great place to find new ideas and fresh optimism. Make it a priority to attend at least one conference each year. Sometimes, the best thing to do is take a break by giving yourself a few weeks off from special events and initiatives.

Don't be discouraged if things don't happen fast. Keep at it, and believe that the message of good character is getting out. Character education is about changing the culture of a school, and that takes time. Developing good character in students takes consistent, creative effort over several years.

Nothing builds excitement as much as results—obvious progress toward a more positive school climate.

Chapter 9

Finding Financial and Other Support

"When we are confident, all we need is a little support."
—*André Laurendeau*

Having money to spend on the character program can increase your options, but it is not essential. You can begin character education with no money at all. Even more important than funding is having a committee that is willing to work together to develop an effective program, and having active, vocal support from your school administration.

In fact, it may be helpful to start the project when you don't have money — that way you'll be encouraged as a committee to use your collective creativity to get the program going. After you've proven what you can do without funds, you're likely to be better stewards of any funding you do receive. As the character project grows, however, you may reach a point where you need additional resources to accomplish the goals you have in mind. At this point, when you're better organized and have a good idea of your objectives, you can begin to look for financial and other support from your school district, business and community partners, and/or institutional grants.

School or District Funds

Your school's operating funds may be available to purchase materials or otherwise support the character program. This is most likely to be true if the school board has requested or approved the program, or if it is mandated at your school. Talk with your school principal, the media specialist, and department heads to find out if monies are available for selected purchases. A key to success here is having a very visible program and good working relationships with other staff members.

The funding myth

It's a popular misconception that you must have funding to have a character program. This is simply not true. Begin with the idea that you do not need money, and do what you can with the resources you have. With enthusiasm and creativity, your program can go a long way toward reaching students with the message of good character. You do not need money to convey this message! Don't use a lack of funding as an excuse not to get started.

Community Donations

As we have said before, local organizations and businesses can be helpful in supporting your character program. Begin by talking with the school's business partners (if you have them), business leaders in your community, and members of civic groups like the Rotary Club or Kiwanis. Local businesses often are keenly interested in supporting programs that help develop more effective future employees. Civic groups are typically service-oriented and interested in the quality of education in their communities. Keep in mind that businesses may find it easier to donate "stuff" rather than money. Their donations can be used to support an incentive program or to provide contest rewards, refreshments for Parents' Night, or items for goodwill projects. Keep your eyes open for all possibilities.

Grants

Many local, state, and federal grants are available to support character education programs. To find out what's available in your area, first check with the grants department in your school or district. (Some districts even have a staff member whose job it is to apply for and oversee grants. If this is true in your district, get to know that person and invite him or her to attend a committee meeting.) If you don't have a grants department, or if the person there isn't helpful, keep going. Use the Web sites listed in the Resource Guide of this book to do your own research. Talk with other schools in your state who have implemented character programs. Finding grants can sometimes seem like detective work. When you find a grant that your school would qualify for, write or call for more information and an application.

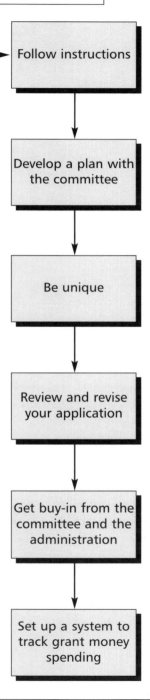

The Grant Writing Process

Determine if your program fits a grant's criteria → Follow instructions

Develop a plan with the committee

Be unique

Review and revise your application

Get buy-in from the committee and the administration

Set up a system to track grant money spending

Don't assume that grant monies will solve your problems, though—they may create new issues. Most grants have strict requirements for application and for management of funds. Writing and managing grants is time-consuming and requires great attention to detail. If your committee is interested in pursing grant funds, identify a committee member who is very conscientious and detail-oriented to handle the record-keeping. It's better if you, the chairperson, are spared this responsibility so your time and energy can be focused on running the program. Grants do provide money that may enable you to accomplish things you might not be able to do otherwise, but they also take a great deal of time.

Writing grants: be systematic and thorough

Writing a grant can seem mysterious and intimidating if you've never written one before. By following a systematic approach, though, you can prepare a useful document that has a good chance of garnering funds for your program.

1. Get a copy of the grant. Write down the criteria being used to award funds. Decide if your project fits within these criteria. If not, don't try to push it—look for funding elsewhere. You'll save yourself and the grant committee tons of time.

2. Follow the grant instructions precisely. Don't skip sections or decide that you don't really need to provide the information as requested. If a section does not apply to you, write "N/A" or otherwise indicate that you have chosen not to complete that section. Don't just leave it blank.

3. Separate out the different sections of the grant and put each section on a huge sheet of paper. At a committee meeting, solicit input from members on each section. Together develop a plan for how you would use the funds for which you are applying. Don't apply until you have a well-developed plan that fits the criteria of the grant. Note that you must be committed to keeping the plan as you have outlined it. Be careful as you write the grant that you can do what you say you are going to do.

4. Put something unique into your grant. This will help your application stand out from the others and may increase your likelihood of receiving funds.

5. Review and revise your grant so that it conveys a clear, concise plan and is professional in appearance. Expect to spend some time fine-tuning the paperwork.

6. Make sure you have buy-in from all committee members and from your administrators. If you receive funding, you will be expected to carry out the plan you have outlined. If you also need district-level approval before submitting the grant, follow up to be sure your hard work is not lost on someone's desk.

7. Finally, set up a system to track your spending. Grants require that you be accountable for the money you spend.

When you prepare a grant application, take care to be professional. Check your grammar and spelling. Double-check your math. Type your application. Respect the grant deadline. Don't scribble a budget in pencil on an index card and expect to be funded!

Self-Funding

Of course, there's always that old stand-by of program funding: the fundraiser! This option is particularly useful for supporting student-initiated events, and your school's student character club may want to explore the different fund-raising methods available. As word of the program gets out in your community and among parents, more and more people will be eager to help support the program. Instead of just selling candy among the students, though, consider a weekend pancake breakfast or other event that could be attended by parents and school neighbors. Don't forget to use your fundraiser to let people know about the good things happening at your school.

As you find financial support for the character program, don't forget to thank the persons or organizations providing the funding. This is such a small step, but it is vitally important; we can't expect students to learn gratitude and appreciation if we don't practice it ourselves. When you obtain donations from local community organizations and businesses, let them know how you are using the funds and the impact those funds are having. When you receive grant monies, take the time to send a note of thanks to the sponsoring organization. This is only courteous. People like to know that the money, goods, and services they donate are being used wisely and are having a positive effect.

Support for the character program will come in many forms. Don't wait until you have money to begin the program.

Chapter 10

Measuring the Effect of Character Education

"Great things are not done by impulse, but by a series of small things brought together."
—*Vincent van Gogh*

Assessing the effect of character education is an important part of the overall program. When the school climate changes, teachers and students alike notice the difference—but how do you quantify this change in objective terms? How do you measure an increase in respect, or honesty, or courtesy? Even though assessment is not always clear-cut, it is a vital activity. The objective data it generates can be very useful for convincing persons outside the school that the character program deserves support. Assessment data can also point out areas where improvement or increased focus is needed. Furthermore, some form of assessment is usually required as a condition of receiving grant monies.

Several tools may be helpful in measuring the impact of your character program. Formal assessment tools can offer objectivity and sound evidence of the program's effectiveness. Customized measures developed specifically by the committee can help you evaluate the success of your unique program. In many cases, a combination of both formal and customized tools is most helpful. Before choosing a measurement technique, however, you must decide what parameters you want to measure.

The task of assessment can be broken down into four distinct steps:
1. Decide what you want to measure.
2. Set appropriate goals.
3. Collect the data.
4. Respond to the measurements.

Choosing What to Measure

As a committee, how will you judge the success of your program? What characteristics do you want to focus on this year? Is it important to see a significant decrease in swearing in the halls, or fewer fights, or a reduction in suspensions? Do you want to concentrate your efforts on increasing student volunteerism and community involvement? It's likely that there are several areas in which committee members would like to see improvement. After you decide what you want to emphasize during the current school year, you can tailor your program activities specifically toward bringing about improvements in those areas. Your focus may be different next year—that's OK, and it's probably a good idea!

Because education is a service-oriented enterprise, measurement is more complex than if you were making gizmos with a uniform size and color. Your "products"—educated, prepared students—are much more personalized. If you think of teaching as a service-oriented business (such as a dentist's office or insurance company), you can see that what you achieve as a teacher can be divided into two types of results: Outcome results and Experience results.

Outcome results

Outcome results are what you do, create, or produce. As a science teacher, your outcome may be students who understand the basic tenets of chemistry, biology, or physics and who are prepared for further study if they so choose. Each teacher has a different set of outcome results, depending on his or her specialty. You also have outcome results as a character committee. Do students have an

Note: To adequately cover the topic of assessment would require many more pages than have been allotted here. Resources are available which contain comprehensive discussions of assessment in relation to character education programs. For more information, refer to the Resource Guide.

Success Tip: It's important to realize that, even in education, we are responsible for the systems we create. If your program is not being effective, it's up to the committee to figure out what could be done differently. Instead of blaming students, parents, or teachers, look for how you can change the program.

increased understanding of what it means to be respectful? Are students more thankful? More honest?

Experience results

Experience results describe the environment one must go through to reach the outcomes. What does it feel like to be at your school? Are teachers excited about going to work in the morning? What do students think of their school? Is learning a struggle because of discipline problems? How about parents—do they perceive the school as being responsive to their needs? When you track experience results, you get a sense of how key stakeholders view the school. You can then work to create the feelings you want those stakeholders to have.

Both outcome and experience results can be tracked in measurable, quantifiable terms, and both are important. Outcome results without experience results, or vice versa, will not give you a true picture of how you are doing.

To determine which aspects of the program you will measure during the year, first decide on the parameters that are most important to you as a committee. You may want to have a brainstorming session to generate the topics, then use multi-voting to narrow down the list. Challenge yourselves, but try to be realistic! Next, check to make sure you're measuring both outcome results and experience results—together they will give you a sense of overall effectiveness. Finally, solicit comments from key stakeholders, particularly teachers and school administrators; your goals may dovetail nicely with other programs and initiatives in the school and provide opportunities for collaboration.

Setting Appropriate Goals

When setting goals for the character program, it's tempting to try to "conquer the world" in the first year. You're more likely to see results, though, if you focus on a few key areas. Being too ambitious can set you up for disappointment and a sense of failure. To this end, it can help to use SMART criteria. This means setting goals that are:

S   Specific
M   Measurable
A   Attainable
R   Relevant
T   Timely

Specific
Choose goals that are concerned with a precise activity. When your goals are vague, you can never be quite sure that you've reached them. For example: Can every student give an example of each character trait in action?

Measurable
Make sure you can measure your goals so you will know when you've met them. For example: Decrease discipline referrals by 25% over the course of the year.

Attainable

Select goals that are attainable, even if they are a stretch. It's great to have goals that challenge you, but goals which are clearly impossible don't motivate anyone. For example, it wouldn't be realistic to have a goal of no discipline referrals in the final quarter of the school year.

Relevant

Make sure the committee's goals are aligned with the school's overall mission. This may seem obvious, but it's important to consider. For example, if your school has a significant problem with tolerance and is addressing the issue in numerous ways, it's a good idea to focus on tolerance in the character program as well.

Timely

Choose specific time frames within which you will accomplish your goals. These can be as short as a month or as long as the school year. With longer-term goals, it's helpful to break them down into more timely "milestones" so you can monitor your progress toward the end result.

Collecting the Data

After you have decided what parameters you want to measure, you can begin to figure out which tools will help you evaluate those parameters. A number of formal assessment instruments can be used to evaluate different parameters of attitude and behavior, such as honesty, moral reasoning, social responsibility, civic attitudes, and others. These tools differ in their structure, ease of use, reliability, and validity. Some assessments are supported by substantial research and testing, while others are not.

In addition to formal assessment tools, you may want to develop your own customized measures of program success. If you can't measure atmosphere, then it's important to figure out what parameters contribute to the school atmosphere and measure those parameters. For example, you may want to track several small but specific items, such as number of fights, suspensions, or other items. While it's true that you can't necessarily tie the character program directly to these outcomes, they do give a sense of the effectiveness of the program in altering the school atmosphere. Graphs can be great tools for displaying these measures. As the character program is implemented, the trends that are illustrated by your graphs will help you evaluate the program.

Using graphs to view the data

Graphs are often used to display data after you've collected it. There are many computer programs available which will graph data for you, but hand-drawn graphs are fine, too. The graphs don't need to be formal to be effective.

To start with, the variable that you want to track (such as number of fights) is placed on the vertical axis of the graph. You will have to decide what units to use for measuring this variable (such as percent, number, etc.). The time unit is placed on the horizontal axis. Will you record the information daily, weekly, or monthly? Make this decision, then mark your graph accordingly. In most cases, the more frequently you can measure and track the variable, the more useful it will be. You may need to collect some preliminary data to determine the best scales to use.

Your next step is to collect baseline data. After you have several data points, calculate the average of your data and draw that average as a solid horizontal line on the chart. By this time, you have probably decided on your goal. You will want to draw this line on the graph as well, perhaps in another color such as red. Continue to add data to the chart as it is collected. If possible, post the chart in a prominent place such as the teacher's lounge or central office. When an unusual event occurs you may want to mark it on the chart to provide a record of the event. Try to include as much information about circumstances as possible; this information will be very helpful when you are looking for trends and trouble-shooting problems.

Responding to the Measurements

Your efforts to assess the effectiveness of the program are of no use unless you respond to what the data are telling you. After all, the whole reason behind assessment is to see what is or is not working and to make improvements. When the results are great, assessment can be very rewarding. In some cases, however, an assessment may suggest that what you are doing is not working.

For example, let's say you conduct a series of assessments evaluating students' attitudes toward peers, teachers, and family members, as a way of measuring respect. If, several months into the program, the data suggest that respect has not increased, you may have a big question to answer. Why haven't your efforts been successful in effecting change in this parameter? You may be tempted to throw up your hands in frustration, saying "Who knows?" Instead of giving up, though, the committee should tackle that question immediately and with as much detachment as possible. Perhaps other problems at the school are clouding the issue. Maybe the way you are measuring is faulty. Perhaps other teachers are not reinforcing the character traits as much as you thought they were. As a committee you will want to examine the problem carefully and thoroughly, then make adjustments in the program.

Assessment can be a gold mine of information, or it can be more paperwork that you dread and avoid at every opportunity. As the chairperson, it may be your role to help the committee move beyond the attitude of "it feels good so it must be working" and toward more objective indications of program effectiveness. Be sure to share assessment results with all the adults in the school. If the results are positive, congratulate and thank them. If the results show areas for improvement, ask for their input in identifying the problems and developing solutions. When teachers and administrators see that the committee is serious about measuring success and improving the program, they will take it more seriously as well.

When assessment is well-done, it gets attention. Armed with carefully collected objective data, you will have another tool for showing that the character program is making a difference in your school.

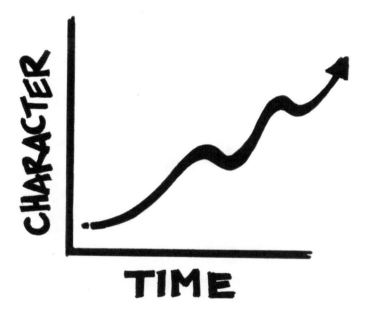

Well-done assessment gets attention for your program.
Assessment tools allow you to quantify the changes you
are seeing in the school climate.

Chapter 11

Improving the Program

"Start by doing what's necessary, then what's possible, and suddenly you are doing the impossible."
—St. Francis of Assisi

The modern business world is built on the idea of continuous improvement—after all, if businesses don't keep improving their products and services, they'll lose customers to the competition. In education, it's easy to get into a rut and do things the same way year after year, regardless of whether a different method would be more effective. Because most character education programs attempt to saturate the environment with the character message, variety is very important. Students will quickly become bored with the same approach and start tuning out the message. In effect, you will have lost your students to the competition.

To keep character education fresh and interesting to students—and therefore effective—you need to continuously improve your program. Two major steps will help bring about improvement: 1) evaluating what you've done, and 2) implementing new ideas.

Evaluating What You've Tried

Make it a habit to evaluate the effectiveness of every program initiative, either as soon as it is completed (for a one-time event) or regularly as you go along (for longer initiatives). The best time to evaluate a one-time event is at the very next character committee meeting; by waiting a few days after the event, you'll have had time to recover from the effort and to collect feedback from students and teachers. Make time on the meeting agenda to discuss the event:

- What went well?
- What could be improved?
- How would we do this event differently next time?

Use the round-robin technique to get everyone involved equally in the discussion. Be sure that the recorder takes good notes for the meeting minutes. You may even want to create an "evaluation sheet" to complete after each initiative to help you remember the particulars of the event.

For longer-term initiatives, such as a year-long focus on a particular character trait, you won't want to wait until the end of the year to evaluate your progress. Add time for program evaluation to the meeting agenda at least once every semester. Ask yourselves:

- What is going well?
- What isn't working?
- What improvements can we make now?
- What changes should we consider for next year?

Continuous improvement is not so much another thing to do as it is a mindset. The companies making the greatest strides in improving their products and services are the ones for whom continuous improvement is a top priority. As you incorporate evaluation and feedback into the way the committee operates, it will become second nature to continuously monitor and improve your program. Until this is habitual, though, it helps to have some guidelines. In a nutshell, you can improve the program by dissecting your successes, by looking for what "wows" students and teachers, and by using a systematic approach to solve problems.

Dissect successes

It feels great when something you've planned is a success. The students have enjoyed themselves and heard your message. Teachers are complimenting the committee on the event. The administrators are pleased. It is tempting to pat yourselves on the back and bask in the glory—but don't miss the learning opportunity. You can learn as much from successes as you can from failures. (Interesting, though, that we rarely reflect on why something was successful.) When your program or event is a success, figure out what made it successful. As a group, identify four or five ingredients that contributed to the success. Note these in the meeting minutes and try to incorporate them when planning future events. Then identify several ways that the event could have been improved further. The next time you plan a similar event, you'll have a clear record of what worked and what could be improved.

Look for the "WOW"

Be aware of which programs, events, and formats create a "WOW" reaction at your school. What things had the greatest impact on students? Which events generated the most excitement among teachers? What grabbed students' attention and held it? You have a lot to compete with in this age of endless streaming media. When something wows your kids, pay attention and learn from it.

Solve the problems

In order for your school's character program to progress from merely "functional" to "highly effective," you may have to do some in-depth problem-solving. This may not be easy, but it is very

> A problem well stated is a problem half solved.
> —Charles F. Kettering

necessary. Significant problems can seriously handicap your school's character program.

Systematic problem-solving

A systematic approach to problem-solving can help the committee be more objective—and more effective—in addressing such problems.

Identify the problem

The first step in problem-solving is to identify the real problem. It can be tempting to jump to conclusions about the problem, making assumptions based on your perceptions and intuition. Sometimes you are right, but other times what you identify as the problem is only a symptom of the real issue. When identifying the problem, ask:

- What is the current situation?
- What do we want the situation to be?
- Do we all agree on the issue?
- Is the problem within the scope of the committee's influence?

To help clarify the problem, it may be useful to write a problem statement. A problem statement identifies the problem and its effect, focusing on the gap between what is and what should be. As much as possible, express the problem in measurable terms. For example, "Our teachers are not supporting the character program" is not a very useful problem statement. A more effective statement is, "Our teachers are not clear on how to incorporate character traits into their daily lessons. As a result, approximately half of our teachers are not reinforcing the program in their classrooms in a meaningful or effective way." This exercise is particularly helpful when there is not clear agreement on the problem; getting it down in writing can help committee members sort through everyone's differing perceptions of the issue and reach consensus.

Use real information to understand the problem

Once you've identified the problem, analyze it from every angle. From the information you have, can you identify root causes of the problem? (If so, list them.) Is the problem occurring regularly or only on certain occasions? If occasional, can you predict when the problem will occur? Could this problem be a symptom of something else? If necessary, take a few weeks to collect information about the extent and nature of the problem. This step is not a waste of time! If you invest time trying to get at the heart of the problem, you're very likely to save time solving the problem.

Think of potential solutions

When you thoroughly understand the problem, start generating potential solutions. Consider inviting someone from outside the committee to attend a meeting and help think of ways to address the problem. An outside perspective can be invaluable in questioning the status quo. Consider as many possible solutions as you can before moving on, even if some of the solutions seem unlikely at first glance.

Implement the best solution

When choosing the best solution, consider how it will affect everyone involved. You may need to analyze the cost of several solutions

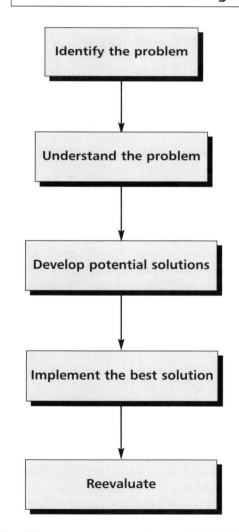

Effective Problem Solving

- Identify the problem
- Understand the problem
- Develop potential solutions
- Implement the best solution
- Reevaluate

Processes, not people

A key attitude needed for effective problem-solving is believing that processes rather than people are at fault. You may find yourself thinking, "This program would be more successful if teachers would do what they say they are going to do," or "This character stuff just doesn't work with the kind of students we have." In fact, business leader and quality expert Dr. Joseph Juran estimated that 85% of problems are caused by inadequate processes, and only 15% of problems are caused by people. Borrowing again from business, consider that a machine operator cannot do a good job using faulty equipment and inadequate tools; similarly, a teacher can't do a thorough job when he or she doesn't know where to begin to incorporate the character trait into a math lesson. When problem-solving, remember to focus on identifying which processes need improvement rather than which people are at fault.

versus the benefits they would bring. Sometimes you might choose the easiest solution first, with the hope that it could mitigate the immediate problem. In many cases, a true solution may require several steps and some time before the problem is finally resolved.

Planning how you will implement the solution is critical to the success of your problem-solving efforts. Many good ideas and intentions amount to nothing without an implementation plan. With a detailed plan of attack and consensus from the committee, changes and improvements can be made in a way that builds teamwork and strengthens the program. Regular communication and "updates" are important to keep committee members informed about the progress of the implementation. And in the case of unexpected events, the committee should be prepared to modify the plan as needed.

Reevaluate the problem

An important but frequently overlooked step in problem-solving is to revisit the problem after you've supposedly "solved" it. Has there been an improvement? Or, are we at least making progress toward our goal? Have any new problems been created by our solution?

Beware of the "middle mile"

You'll want to watch out for what's called the "middle mile." After you've pursued a character program for a while, you may find yourselves at a point where it looks like you are not accomplishing anything, and everyone is weary of the effort. This often occurs at the halfway point, where the excitement has waned and the goal is still somewhere in the future. Over and over, experience has shown that it takes five years to effectively turn a school around. This does not mean that there are no results for five years—just that the really big "wins" are not usually evident at the beginning. As chairperson, here is where you will want to keep the vision alive for the committee by remaining optimistic and reminding them of the accomplishments to date.

Implementing New Ideas

Implementing new ideas is another important aspect of continuous improvement. At least once per year, have an "outside the box" meeting, where the focus is solely on generating fresh approaches for the program—thinking beyond the way you've always done things. Ask everyone on the committee to come to the meeting with at least two new ideas to discuss. There are many places to find ideas; as your experience with teaching character grows, you'll start seeing potential ideas everywhere. A few suggestions:

Look at your data
The data you collect as part of the program assessment can lead you toward new ideas. What are the data telling you? Are students hearing the message but not acting on it? Are teachers tired of the current program structure? Are parents feeling like the character message is not coming home with their children? Feedback from others can suggest areas for renewed focus or a change in emphasis.

> Let us then be up and doing,
> With a heart for any fate,
> Still achieving, still pursing,
> Learn to labor and to wait.
> —Henry Wadsworth
> Longfellow

Beg, borrow, and ... adapt

Talk with teachers at other schools that are incorporating character lessons. Share ideas. Adapt something which has worked at their school to fit the culture of yours. Reading professional journals, going to conferences, and using Internet resources can result in many new ideas. Use email to ask questions of other teachers who are implementing character programs. Many schools in the U.S. are traveling on this path—there's no reason for any of us to think that we have to figure it all out by ourselves.

Talk to other teachers at your school. Teachers who aren't on the character committee may nonetheless have terrific ideas about the program. You are asking them to join with you in the initiative, so it makes sense to solicit their input regularly. Make it easy for other teachers to be involved, even if tangentially. If a teacher mentions an idea that strikes a cord, invite him or her to present the idea to the committee. If you decide to implement the idea, give the person who thought of it a chance to be further involved and see the idea through. You may pick up a new committee member in the process.

Recruit new committee members

Finally, keep bringing in fresh ideas by welcoming new people to the committee. After a while, all of us get tired and less able to think in new ways. Someone who is new to the committee, and particularly someone who is new to the school, is less likely to be stuck in a rut that may have become comfortable for everyone else.

Continuous improvement will help keep the character program fresh and attractive to students and staff.

Chapter 12

Optimizing Committee Dynamics

"A character educator is like an art instructor who works on his own art while helping others become artists."
— *Kevin Ryan & Karen Bohlin, <u>Building Character in Schools</u>*

One characteristic affects the success of your character program more than anything else: the ability of the committee to work together effectively. It may take some time to optimize interpersonal dynamics among committee members, but the reward will be a group that is fun to be involved with and one that accomplishes much.

Understanding several important concepts can help the group become a great team. Keeping discussions effective will help increase the productivity of your meetings. Knowing how to give and receive feedback, and doing it, helps generate good will among members and avoid misunderstandings. Understanding and appreciating committee members' different behavioral styles can help you take advantage of member strengths and reduce problems with interpersonal dynamics. Dealing appropriately with group problems can help keep the committee healthy and productive. Finally, recognizing normal patterns of team development can help you remain optimistic even in the midst of apparent chaos in team dynamics.

Keeping Discussions Effective

An important component of working well together as a committee is knowing how to have effective discussions. This is not as simple as it may seem! It takes both patience and courtesy to listen carefully so you hear what others are saying—even if they don't express themselves clearly. It takes courage to keep the discussion focused on the topic, to read and respond to body language, and to solicit input from more quiet members. It takes resolve to keep track of time, to avoid talking a subject to death, and to encourage consensus. By applying these important techniques, though, meeting productivity will increase and committee members are likely to feel more satisfied with their contributions to the group.

Listen

How many times in a meeting do you find yourself forming your response to the other person (often about how his or her idea won't work) rather than really listening to what is being said? Try to actively explore ideas rather than debating them or detailing why they won't work. Some of your committee members will be good at thinking big, and others will be good at making ideas practical. Encourage a healthy synthesis between these two points of view.

Focus

Distraction and digression are the enemies of effective discussion. Expect everyone to give the meeting their full attention, and do your best to keep the group focused on the topic at hand. Make it clear that committee members should not be interrupted by outside issues during the meeting except in true emergencies. You can do this by adhering to the "100-mile rule": no one should be interrupted unless the disruption would occur even if you were 100 miles from the school. If side issues are taking attention away from the agenda, don't hesitate to call the committee back to the topic. Also, don't permit overly long examples or irrelevant discussion to eat up your meeting time. As much as possible, maintain focus.

Read body language

People say so much without uttering a word. Learn to read your committee members' non-verbal cues. Looking around, shifting in their seats, grimacing slightly, clenching the jaw—all these tell you how people are feeling about the way a meeting is going. When you sense dissatisfaction, don't be afraid to confront the problem. You might say, for example, "I can see that people are getting tired of talking about this. Should we table the issue until the next meeting?"

Encourage equal participation

It's your job to manage the discussions so that certain persons don't dominate while other persons say nothing. If needed, solicit the opinions of less aggressive committee members by asking them directly for input. One technique for doing this is to take a "temperature check": go around the group and ask each person in turn for his or her opinion or ideas on a subject. If one person is dominating, you can say, "OK, I think we know how Don feels about this issue. What about everyone else? Let's do a temperature check so we can move toward consensus."

Keep track of time

It's important, for group morale, to feel like progress is being made during the meeting. If a particular topic is taking longer than you've allowed in the agenda, remind the group of the time constraints and actively decide whether you will continue with the subject or move on to the other agenda items. Consider asking someone to fill the role of timekeeper.

Don't beat a dead horse

Sometimes we can talk and talk about an issue without getting anywhere. It may be necessary to end a discussion where nothing is being gained. In such cases, either make a decision with the information you have or postpone the decision until another meeting. Continuing to restate the issue—to beat the dead horse—casts a pall of negativity over the meeting and demoralizes everyone.

Summarize

From time to time, summarize what's been said or decided and restate it to the group. Follow that with a question: "Do I have it right?" or "Is there anything I've missed?" If you're on track, ask the recorder to note the decision in the meeting minutes. It may be helpful to write it on a flip chart as well.

Check for consensus

After summarizing the discussion on a subject, check to see if the committee is in agreement on the issue. You might say, "Do we have consensus on how we will proceed?" or "Does anyone disagree with what's been decided?" It's always better to state the obvious than to assume everyone agrees, only to find out later that the group was really not in agreement.

Positive-Interesting-Negative (PIN)

Even if you don't like a particular suggestion, try to respond using the PIN method: Positive, Interesting, Negative. With each idea, first discuss the positive aspects of the idea, then the interesting aspects, and finally the negative. You should lead the committee in establishing this kind of rapport among its members.

Using Feedback

Feedback is another cornerstone of team development. The most effective committees are ones where people talk to each other—honestly, openly, and often. Four basic types of feedback govern interactions: silence, criticism, constructive feedback, and appreciative feedback. Silence, or lack of response, is in itself a form of feedback. While silence is the least confrontational form of feedback, it is also the least effective. At best, silence maintains the status quo; at worst, it leads to misunderstanding and tension within the group. Criticism is another ineffective form of feedback. It is usually easier to be critical than to listen and consider another person's ideas when they differ from your own. Criticism usually becomes personal very quickly and can lead the group into a negative spiral of defensiveness and counter-criticism. Avoid silence and criticism in the group at all costs!

For optimal communication, help the group learn to give and receive constructive and appreciative feedback. Constructive feedback focuses on what is positive about an idea or a behavior without ignoring what is less than optimal. For example: "Bob, I like your idea about including students in the fund-raiser. I'm concerned, though, about the liability issues. What could we do to avoid those?" Another example: "Janet, your enthusiasm is wonderful, and it really helps me feel excited about the project. You can come on strong sometimes, though, and people seem to be intimidated by you. Have you noticed that?"

Appreciative feedback identifies and praises positive qualities about other persons or their ideas. Liberal use of appreciative feedback increases goodwill among committee members and encourages teamwork. Appreciative feedback also increases the effectiveness of constructive feedback—when you're told frequently that you are doing things well, you're more likely to listen when told about something you could improve.

Giving feedback

Knowing when and how to give feedback is an important part of communication. To know if your timing is right, you should consider both yourself and the person receiving the feedback. You shouldn't give feedback if your purpose is to put the person on the spot or to demonstrate your superiority, or if the time, place, or circumstances are not appropriate.

Consider the following guidelines when offering feedback to another person.

Be descriptive

Specific statements are more useful than general statements. If you tell others exactly what you think the problem is, they are better able to prevent it in the future. Similarly, if you tell them exactly what they did well, they will probably try to repeat that in the future. Also, show how specific actions created positive (or negative) results. It's helpful to know how your efforts fit in with the larger whole.

Be timely

Constructive feedback usually should be given in private. Furthermore, ask permission before giving this type of feedback. If the person is having a bad day, he or she might prefer to hear what you have to say at another time. Give feedback as close to the event as possible. Feedback is less effective if you wait several days or weeks to deliver it.

Be supportive

Rather than telling someone that they have a problem and should go fix it, you need to offer support in finding a solution.

Focus on "I" rather than "You"

Using "I" statements rather than "you" statements helps people be less defensive when receiving your feedback. Resist the urge to say things like, "You are irresponsible." These statements cause people to become defensive and miss your message.

Don't overstate the facts

Statements such as, "You are always late for the meeting," will cause the person to argue rather than to hear what you are saying. Avoid superlatives like "always," "never," and "every."

Avoid third-party feedback

Don't let yourself be caught in other people's hidden agendas. For example, the statement "I've heard that you are not supporting the committee in your department" is likely to cause distrust and hard feelings. Third-party feedback is unfair both to you and to the person you are addressing. Give feedback only about what you have observed yourself.

Receiving feedback

How you react to feedback is just as important as how you give it. When reacting:

Listen carefully

Chances are there's a kernel of truth buried somewhere in the feedback. Listen to what is being said, and try to discern the real issue underneath the words and emotion. Try not to interrupt, which could discourage the person giving you feedback. (On the other hand, you don't have to stand there and let yourself be berated. It's important to distinguish an honest attempt at feedback from a personal attack.)

Breathe deeply

When stressed, we have physiological reactions such as an increased heart rate and shallow breathing. When you are receiving unexpected feedback, remember to breathe deeply and stay calm.

Clarify information

If you don't understand what is being said, say so. It's definitely not productive to listen to someone's feedback and go away not understanding their comments. This only leads to deepening divisions and the attitude of "He/she doesn't like me." Ask for examples if you need to. After you understand clearly what the person is saying, then you can decide what you are willing to do about it.

Acknowledge the feedback and its valid points

Acknowledge that the person has come to you with their feedback, in whatever form, and thank them for doing so. Also acknowledge the valid points being offered. If you were wrong, admit it—the more you admit your mistakes, the more you encourage others to do the same. Fostering an open environment among committee members starts with you, the chairperson.

Think about it

If you need to, take some time to calm down and think about how best to respond. If you cannot discuss the topic productively at the time of the feedback, then schedule another time to follow up with the person. Just be sure that you do follow up within the next day or so.

Understanding Behavioral Styles

To be effective in committee situations, it can help to have a basic understanding of behavioral styles. Being able to adapt to different styles of behavior is a key skill for teachers to develop. Our habitual response when working with someone is to observe that person's behavior (usually for just a short while), draw conclusions based on the behavior, and then react out of habit. When a person displays a style we are comfortable with, we tend to react positively, thinking that he or she is "like us." If a person displays behaviors we are uncomfortable with, we tend to withdraw and be more guarded. It is more effective, though, to observe a person's behavioral style, draw conclusions based on your knowledge of the different styles, and then adapt to that style.

Assertiveness

Ask ←――――――――――――――――――→ **Tell**

You can be a more effective committee chairperson by being aware of natural differences in how people behave.

There are a number of different assessments that social scientists use to categorize people's styles of behavior. A well-known assessment used in business is the Behavioral Styles Inventory®, which categorizes assertiveness and responsiveness dimensions of behavior.

Assertiveness

Assertiveness can be defined as the extent to which we attempt to influence the thoughts and actions of others. This can be illustrated as a horizontal line, representing a continuum, with "Tell assertive" behavior on the right side of the line and "Ask assertive" behavior on the left side of the line, as shown above.

Arrows are drawn on the line because we don't stay at one point on the continuum; every day we adapt in our assertiveness along this line, depending on the persons we are with and the situation. If we are making a presentation to parents, for example, we are not likely to be as assertive as we might be with students. And even though we move along this line, we all have a default style where we are most comfortable. While this "zone" may be comfortable for us, it may not always represent the most effective response to a given situation.

Certain behaviors displayed by your committee members will give you clues to whether they are more comfortable in a "Tell assertive" or an "Ask assertive" mode. Tell assertive types tend to be fast-paced risk-takers

Responsiveness

Control

Emote

who make statements, particularly "I" statements; these people are comfortable taking charge and are typically verbal. In contrast, Ask assertive types tend to be laid-back, cautious, and cooperative; they are more likely to ask questions and to go along. They tend to be less verbal.

Responsiveness

The other dimension of behavior assessed by the Behavioral Styles Inventory® is responsiveness, defined as the degree to which we display our feelings in professional situations. This scale can be represented by a vertical line, with "Control response" at one end of the line and "Emote response" at the other end, as shown to the right. Note that this scale does not consider whether we have emotions—because we all do—but rather how we handle those emotions in public. People who prefer "Control response" behavior seldom display their emotions in work situations. Persons who prefer the "Emote response" behavior are more likely to "wear their feelings" outwardly.

Again, arrows represent the fact that we move among this line depending on the situation. As with assertiveness, behaviors displayed by committee members will help you understand whether they are more comfortable with a "Control response" or an "Emote response." You will be wise to adapt your approach to meet them where they are most comfortable, even if it means a stretch for you.

Persons who are most comfortable with a "Control response" are likely to be described as conservative, calm, cool, or "all business." These persons are not likely to show strong emotions and may seem very disciplined.

Persons who are more comfortable with an "Emote response" may be described as excitable, expressive, social, or warm. They are more likely to be spontaneous and to display their feelings publicly.

When we combine the two scales, they form a four-quadrant matrix which can be used to classify behavior:

Tell-assertive and Control-responsive	=	**Driver**
Tell-assertive and Emote-responsive	=	**Expressive**
Ask-assertive and Emote-responsive	=	**Amiable**
Ask-assertive and Control-responsive	=	**Analytical**

As shown in the matrix on the following page, each behavioral style can be characterized with descriptive terms that help predict how persons with that style will typically behave. For example, assume that the committee is trying to make a decision about a difficult issue. The "Driver" on your committee is likely to be the first to say, "All right, we've talked this to death. Let's get on with it." An "Analytical" will try to pin down the information needed to make a decision. The "Amiable" is likely to suggest compromises between opposing views. The "Expressive" may want to talk about the issue at length.

Behavioral "style"

A person's behavioral style is basically the habitual way in which he or she responds to situations. These habits develop over a long period of time and are not likely to fundamentally change. In some

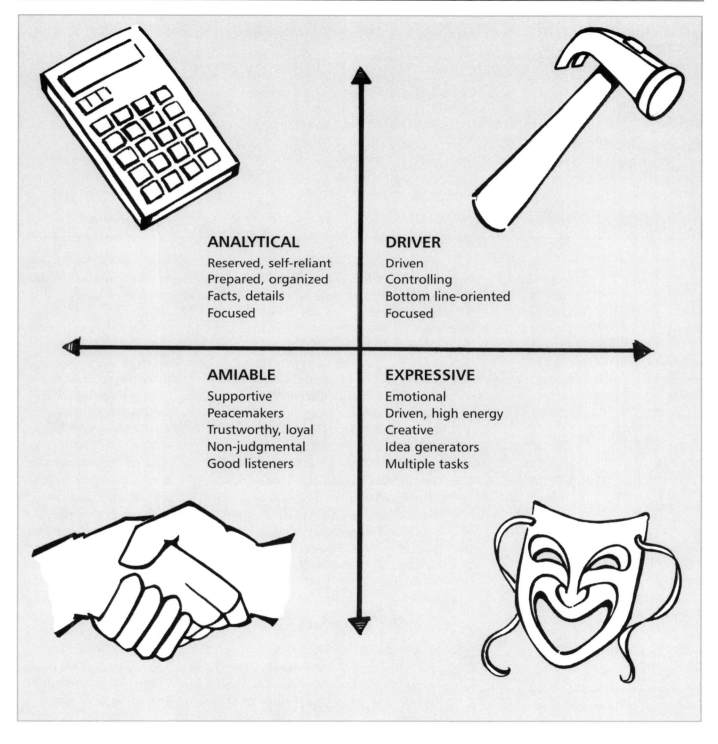

ANALYTICAL
Reserved, self-reliant
Prepared, organized
Facts, details
Focused

DRIVER
Driven
Controlling
Bottom line-oriented
Focused

AMIABLE
Supportive
Peacemakers
Trustworthy, loyal
Non-judgmental
Good listeners

EXPRESSIVE
Emotional
Driven, high energy
Creative
Idea generators
Multiple tasks

> Problems are only opportunities in work clothes.
> —Henry J. Kaiser

situations, however, clinging to a particular style may be ineffective; it can benefit you to behave differently. Being able to move outside of your default zone helps you be more effective in committee situations.

Furthermore, we tend to judge persons whose style differs from our own. For example, it usually doesn't take us long to decide whether we like someone or not, often based on some small behavior that he or she displays or doesn't display. We generally want to be with people who behave as we do. To be most effective on a committee, though, you have to view behaviors that are different from your own as just that: different, not better or worse.

The next step is to adapt ourselves, within reason, to the other person. We can adapt to each other if we want to. In fact, we adapt to each other all the time. If you have a friend who is always very punctual, for example, you probably try hard to make it to your lunch date with that person on time. The same premise works in committee situations—by adapting to each other's needs, you foster a more effective working relationship.

Conflict behaviors

Understanding behavior styles can also help you learn to predict how individuals will react to conflict, thereby allowing you to respond to those situations more effectively. Persons with different behavioral styles handle conflict in vastly different manners. Generally speaking, the following "conflict behaviors" hold true.

CONFLICT BEHAVIORS

ANALYTICAL: *Avoids*

- Focuses attention on detail
- Becomes defensive if pressured
- Displays negative body language

DRIVER: *Becomes autocratic*

- Becomes uncompromising
- Increases voice volume
- Changes the rules

AMIABLE: *Acquiesces*

- Withdraws
- Becomes impatient/inattentive
- Defers

EXPRESSIVE: *Attacks*

- Displays emotion
- Expresses judgment
- May make personal attacks

During conflict, persons who are Ask assertive (i.e., Analytical and Amiable) will display FLIGHT behaviors. You may have to intervene and draw out their feelings. Tell assertive persons (i.e., Driver and Expressive), on the other hand, will display FIGHT behaviors. You may need to let them vent. Then, in both cases, take definite steps to deal with the problem. By responding to conflict behaviors appropriately, you can help build a more effective committee.

Dealing with group problems

Occasionally you may have a situation in which a member or an issue is significantly disrupting the group. If this is the case, be prepared to do something to help resolve the problem. One of the best ways to deal with problems is to prevent them in the first place. Consider time spent developing the group into a team as an investment in future effectiveness. Also, view each problem as a group problem; many issues arise because the group lets them happen. Focus on the system, not the person. Finally, react appropriately to each problem. Some disruptions are fleeting and will have no long-term effect on the group; don't overreact to these situations. Other issues can seriously hamper the committee's progress unless they are resolved; take steps to deal with such situations promptly.

Recognizing Patterns of Team Development

You can't throw a disparate group of people together and expect them to function effectively as a team right away. Most teams go through a predictable pattern of development, and it can be helpful to know what to expect. Well-run groups typically begin with a formation stage, then establish group norms, learn how to manage their conflicts, and finally become effective.

Forming as a team

Initially, the committee will be forming. Committee members need time to get comfortable with the structure and purpose of the group. At this stage members often have unrealistic expectations and some anxiety about being part of the group. They may respond with silence or by being reactive to the chairperson and other members. Structure is important during the early meetings, and you may have to be highly directive in order to get things accomplished. You can help reduce uncertainty by explaining the goals and purpose of the group and by providing time for questions. Take care to model the behaviors you expect from committee members, and pay attention to your nonverbal signals.

Establishing group norms

In the second phase of team development, the group is figuring out how it will operate as a committee: in other words, what are its norms? At this stage committee members will look to you for both support and direction. Reality is setting in: they may find out that things are harder to accomplish than they first thought. You may observe a lack of focus and failure to commit to action plans, along with physical or psychological withdrawal from the group (by being absent, for example). Power struggles may emerge. You can help the group get through this stage by working to develop mutual goals, by encouraging consensus for decision-making, and by modeling positive listening skills. You may have to redirect questions and challenges to reduce hostilities.

Learning to manage conflict

In the third stage of team development, committee members are figuring out how they will manage conflict. During this stage, committee members may increasingly test the group norms, polarize into factions, and even attack each other or the chairperson. You can help the group by reinforcing positive conflict resolution strategies, by not becoming authoritarian, and by recognizing differences of opinion as part of a healthy committee. The members need less direction from you but much support as they embrace the challenges of really participating in the committee's work.

Becoming effective

As your committee becomes an effective team, you will probably breathe a sigh of relief. Committee members will trust one another and listen well. They will be able to give each other feedback in positive, constructive ways. The group will take advantage of different members' strengths and be able to resolve conflicts on their own. Your role in supporting and directing the team's progress may lessen as committee members become responsible and accountable for the committee's work.

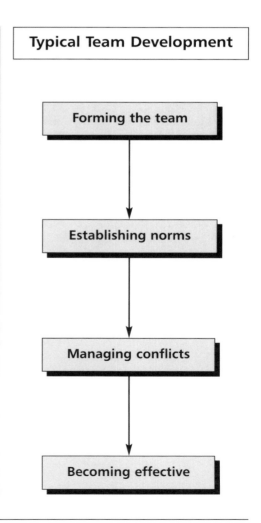

Typical Team Development

Forming the team

Establishing norms

Managing conflicts

Becoming effective

It may take all year to reach the stage of an effective, performing team. Don't despair! This is normal. Keep in mind, too, that any time the group is changed by adding a new member or losing an existing member, the dynamics will change as well. A committee that was performing well may suddenly be back at the forming or norming stages. What you will find, though, is that you move through the various stages more quickly the second or third time around. This is because most of the committee members have had the experience of being part of a great committee and have acquired the skills necessary to help the group move forward.

Optimizing committee dynamics takes time and attention, but it can contribute significantly to the overall effectiveness of the character program.

Post Script

With determination and effort, character education can be a tremendous success at your school. Furthermore, embarking on a character program can bring excitement and encouragement into your life as a teacher. Seeing students change and mature is a great reward. You will know that your hard work is truly making a difference—not only in their lives, but in the lives of the people they touch.

The years you spend on the character committee can be the most exciting in your career. They will bring challenge, self-examination, exhaustion, and exhilaration. You will make new friends, develop your creativity, work with different kinds of people, and learn new skills. You will have the opportunity to grow, to become a leader, to think outside the box, to do a paradigm shift. Your life may become so full that it's overflowing. There's no thrill like being successful at something you believe in. Consider the following poem as your personal challenge:

Nothing in the world
Can take the place of persistence.
Talent will not;
Nothing is more common
Than unsuccessful people with talent.
Genius will not;
Unrewarded genius is almost a proverb.
Education will not;
The world is full of educated derelicts.
Persistence and determination
Alone are important.

Calvin Coolidge

Anne C. Dotson
Cleveland, Ohio

Resource Guide

Authors' Note:
Many great resources are available to help you teach character. Some materials may be labelled for character education, but many others will fall into less specific categories. The list of resources that follows is not intended as a comprehensive listing of all the resources available in character education. Instead, we have cited the organizations and materials with which we are most familiar. As the momentum in character education continues to build, more and more resources will become available.

Books Related to Character

Abourjilie, Charlie. *Developing Character for Classroom Success*. Chapel Hill, NC: Character Development Publishing, 2000.

Bennett, W.J., Ed. *The Book of Virtues: A Treasury of Great Moral Stories*. New York: Simon and Schuster, 1993.

Covey, Stephen R. *The 7 Habits of Highly Effective People*. New York: Simon and Schuster, 1987.

DeRoche, E.F. and Williams, M. *Educating Hearts and Minds: A Comprehensive Character Education Framework*. Thousand Oaks, CA: Corwin Press, 1998.

Dotson, Anne C. and Wisont, Karen D. *Teaching Character: A Teacher's Idea Book*. Chapel Hill, NC: Character Development Group, 1997.

Dotson, Anne C. and Wisont, Karen D. *Teaching Character: Parents' Guide*. Chapel Hill, NC: Character Development Group, 1997.

Kilpatrick, William. *Why Johnny Can't Tell Right From Wrong*. New York: Simon and Schuster, 1992.

Kirchenbaum, H. *100 Ways to Enhance Values and Morality in Schools and Youth Settings*. Boston: Allyn and Bacon, 1995.

Lickona, Thomas. *Educating for Character: How Our Schools Can Teach Respect and Responsibility*. New York: Bantam Books, 1991.

Lickona, Thomas. *Raising Good Children*. New York: Bantam Books, 1983.

Ryan, Kevin and Bohlin, Karen E. *Building Character in Schools*. San Francisco, CA: Jossey-Bass Publishers, 1999.

Urban, Hal. *Life's Greatest Lessons: 20 Things I Want My Kids to Know*. Redwood City, CA: Great Lessons Press, 2000.

Vessels, Gordon G. *Character and Community Development: A School Planning and Teacher Training Handbook*. Westport, CT: Praeger Publishers, 1998.

Curriculum Guides

Caring Habit of the Month. (Middle grades) Comprehensive program emphasizing habits that demonstrate caring.

Available from: All of Us, 305 Furnace Drive, Zelienople, PA 16063; Phone/Fax: 724-453-0447. Email: allofus@icubed.com

Character Counts! (Grades 1-8) Comprehensive program with emphasis on six "pillars" of character: trustworthiness, respect, responsibility, fairness, caring, and citizenship.

    Available from: CHARACTER COUNTS! National Office/ Josephson Institute of Ethics, 4640 Admiralty Way, Suite 1001, Marina del Rey, CA 90292-6610; Phone: 310-306-1868; Fax: 310-827-1864. http://www.charactercounts.org

The Giraffe Heroes Program. (Grades K-12) Story-based curriculum that focuses on people who are willing to stick their necks out for others and help solve tough problems.

    Available from: The Giraffe Project, P.O. Box 759, Langley, WA 98260; Phone: 360-221-7989. http://www.giraffe.org

Heartwood: An Ethics Curriculum for Children. (Pre-K through elementary grades) Ethics curriculum using multi-cultural literature; focuses on universal values including honesty, courage, loyalty, justice, respect, hope, and love.

    Available from: Heartwood Institute, 425 North Craig Street, Suite 302, Pittsburg, PA 15213; Phone: 800-HEART-10. http://www.heartwoodethics.org/

Jefferson Center for Character Education. (Grades K-12) Curricula and training for teachers and parents to teach children the concepts, skills, and behavior of good character, core values, and personal and civic responsibility.

    Available from: 2700 East Foothill Boulevard, Suite 302, Pasadena, CA 91107; Phone: 818-792-8130. http://www.jeffersoncenter.org/

Proud to be Polite. (Grades K-6, high school) Classroom program that uses various media to teach manners and respectful behavior.

> Available from: Proud To Be Polite, P.O. Box 290116, Columbia, SC 29229-0116. Phone: 803-736-1934; Fax: 803-736-0673. http://www.proudtobepolite.com

WiseSkills. (Grades K-8) Interdisciplinary character-building program using the words and lives of great world figures. Focus is on character education, career awareness, and community service.

> Available from: WiseSkills, P.O. Box 491, Santa Cruz, CA 95061; Phone: 888-947-3754. http://www.wiseskills.com/

Publications

The Character Educator. Quarterly publication from The Character Education Partnership (CEP).

> Available from: CEP, 918 16th Street, NW, Suite 501, Washington, DC 20006. Fax: 202-296-7779.

Fourth and Fifth Rs. Bimonthly publication from The Center for the 4th and 5th Rs.

> Available from: Center for the Fourth and Fifth Rs, SUNY Cortland, P.O. Box 2000, Cortland, NY 13045; Phone: 607-753-2455.

Cooperating School Districts. *Evaluation Resource Guide: Tools and Strategies for Evaluating a Character Education Program.* 1999. Comprehensive overview of assessment tools and techniques for use with character education programs.

Available from: Cooperating School Districts of Greater St. Louis, Inc., 8225 Florissant Road, St. Louis, MO 63121. Phone: 314-516-4500. http://info.csd.org/staffdev/chared/prep.html

Kenan Institute for Ethics. *North Carolina Character Educators of the Year: The NCCEY Awards Program*. 2000. Resource book containing character-related lessons for elementary, middle, and high school students; all lessons are winners of NCCEY Awards.

Available from: Kenan Institute for Ethics, 102 West Duke Building, Box 90432, Duke University, Durham, NC 27708; Phone: 919-660-3033. http://kenan.ethics.duke.edu

Organizations and Websites

Center for the Advancement of Ethics and Character (CAEC)
http://www.bu.edu/education/caec/
A research and professional development institute at Boston University for scholars, graduate students, and teachers who want to be better prepared for fostering the character development of their students. Sponsors courses, conferences, lectures, and fieldwork in the area of character education.

Center for the 4th and 5th Rs
http://www.cortland.edu/www/c4n5rs/
A nonprofit organization serving as a regional, state, and national resource in character education. The Center provides character-related articles and sponsors an annual summer institute in character education. The "4th and 5th Rs" are respect and responsibility.

Center for Youth Issues (CYI)

http://www.cyi-stars.org/Default.htm

A non-profit organization that supplies character education materials and training for schools, youth organizations, parents, and community groups. CYI is home of STARS (Students Taking A Right Stand), a student-led, teacher-facilitated support and counseling program.

Character Development Group

Email: Respect96@aol.com

Educator resource organization offering publications and staff development training in character education. Provides workshops, workbooks, textbooks, and other materials.

The Character Education Partnership (CEP)

http://www.character.org/

A nonprofit coalition of organizations and persons dedicated to developing moral character and civic virtue in youth. CEP is an umbrella organization for U.S. character education efforts and provides a National Resource Center. The website contains links to hundreds of character-related sites.

Character Press

http://www.teachingcharacter.com/

Source for articles and books by the authors of *The Character Education Handbook*.

Cooperating School Districts of Greater St. Louis

http://info.csd.org/staffdev/chared/characterplus.html

Cooperative project of more than 30 public school districts in the St. Louis, Missouri region. The CHARACTER*plus* program integrates character education into all aspects of the school.

International Center for Character Education (ICCE), University of San Diego

http://www.acusd.edu/continuing_education/ICCE/
Offers training courses, workshops, certification, and other resources for character education, with emphasis on home, school, church, and community.

Josephson Institute of Ethics

http://www.charactercounts.org
Coalition of schools, communities, and nonprofit organizations working to advance character education by teaching the Character Counts! curriculum.

Kenan Ethics Program, Duke University

http://kenan.ethics.duke.edu/
Supports the study and teaching of ethics, and promotes moral reflection and commitment in personal, professional, community, and civic life. Encourages moral inquiry and reflection across intellectual disciplines and professions.

National Professional Resources

http://www.nprinc.com
Offers professional development and parent training materials in the field of character education.

Ohio Partners in Character Education
http://www.charactereducationohio.org
Statewide coalition of public, non-profit, and private organizations whose goal is to foster character education in the state of Ohio.

Partners for Citizenship & Character (PCC)
http://www.worthington.org/
An association of parents, students, educators, business leaders, and other community members in Worthington, Ohio. Website provides examples of how this community is working together to incorporate principles of good character.

The School for Ethical Education (SEE)
http://www.ethicsed.org/
Offers strategies for putting ethics into action. SEE provides training and consulting in the integration of ethics and character into academic settings.

Order Form

Fax Orders: 925.335.9047 (fax this form)
Phone Orders: 888.280.4390
Email Orders: orders@teachingcharacter.com
Postal Orders: Character Press, P.O. Box 110356, Cleveland, Ohio 44111

Book Title	Quantity	Price	Subtotal
The Character Education Handbook		$29.95	

Subtotal _____

Ohio Residents, please add _____ $2.10 (per book) _____

Shipping _____

Total _____

Shipping	
Book Rate:	$2.30 for 1st book
	+ .50 per addn'l book
Priority:	$4.30 for 1st book
	+ .90 per addn'l book

Payment method: ☐ Check ☐ Credit card
                       ☐ P.O # _____

Credit card information: ☐ Visa ☐ Mastercard

Card number: _____

Name on card: _____ **Exp date:** _____

Ship to:

Name: _____

School (or affiliation): _____

Address: _____

City: _____ **State:** _____ **Zip code:** _____

Telephone: _____

email address: _____